CONDUCTING AND REHEARSING
ORTHODOX LITURGICAL MUSIC

In Memory of

my uncle,

George Lukashevich

(+ 2003),

and

Dedicated to

Nadia Koblosh.

Conducting and Rehearsing Orthodox Liturgical Music

BY

DAVID BARRETT

FOREWARD BY

FATHER SERGEI GLAGOLEV

ORTHODOX LITURGICAL PRESS

SOUTHBURY, CONNECTICUT

JULY 2016

Library of Congress Cataloging-in-Publication Data

Barrett, David
1956 –

   Conducting and Rehearsing Orthodox Liturgical Music

   Library of Congress Control Number: 2015932309

CONDUCTING AND REHEARSING
ORTHODOX LITURGICAL MUSIC

Copyright © 2016 by
David Barrett

Orthodox Liturgical Press
Southbury, CT 06488

All Rights Reserved.

ISBN 978-0-9915905-3-7

Printed in the United States of America.

CONTENTS

FOREWORD xiii

PREFACE xv

I. CONDUCTING ORTHODOX LITURGICAL MUSIC 1

1. SPIRITUAL AND LITURGICAL PREPARATION 3

    A. SPIRITUAL PREPARATION 3

    B. LITURGICAL PREPARATION 12

2. POSTURE, BREATHING, AND TONE PLACEMENT 17

    A. POSTURE 17

    B. BREATHING 18

    C. TONE PLACEMENT 22

    EXERCISES • CHAPTER 2 24

3. TRIADIC HARMONY 29
   - A. MAJOR SCALES 30
   - B. SCALE DEGREES 33
   - C. KEYS AND KEY SIGNATURES 35
   - D. SOLFEGE SYLLABLES 38
   - E. MINOR KEYS AND SCALES 40
   - F. CHORDS AND TRIADS 44
   - G. QUALITIES OF INTERVALS AND TRIADS 47
   - H. 7TH CHORDS 53
   - I. INVERSIONS 54
   - J. TRIADS IN MAJOR AND MINOR KEYS 58
   - K. MUSIC ANALYSIS 59
   - EXERCISES • CHAPTER 3 66

4.	GIVING PITCHES	73
	A. TRIADS	75
	B. INVERSIONS	83
	C. 7TH CHORDS	84
	EXERCISES • CHAPTER 4	85
5.	MELODY AND HARMONY	87
	A. MOTIVES AND PHRASES	87
	B. ANTECEDENT – CONSEQUENT PHRASES	89
	C. MONOPHONY	90
	D. DIOPHONY	92
	E. HOMOPHONY	93
	F. POLYPHONY	94
	EXERCISES • CHAPTER 5	95
6.	CONDUCTING THE CHOIR	97
	A. BEAT PATTERNS	99
	B. CHANT STYLE	103
	C. STIKHERA STYLE	112
	EXERCISES • CHAPTER 6	117

II. REHEARSING ORTHODOX LITURGICAL MUSIC — 119

7. BEGINNING THE CHOIR REHEARSAL — 121
- A. OPENING PRAYER — 122
- B. WARM – UP EXERCISES — 124
- C. PRE – SERVICE WARM – UP — 136
- D. DICTION EXERCISES — 138

8. LITURGICAL AWARENESS AND MUSICAL AWARENESS — 143
- A. LITURGICAL AWARENESS — 143
- B. MUSICAL AWARENESS — 152

9. REHEARSAL TECHNIQUES — 161
- A. INITIAL PREPARATION — 161
- B. FIRST RUN – THROUGH — 165
- C. FINE TUNING — 169
- D. POSITIVE REINFORCEMENT — 173
- E. PHRASING — 176

    F. WOODSHEDDING　　　　　　180

10. LITURGICAL TEAMWORK　　　　221
    A. "... DECENTLY AND IN ORDER!"　　222
    B. THE MAIN CELEBRANT AS THE REFERENCE POINT　　223
    C. THE LITURGICAL BLESSING　　224
    D. CONSTRUCTIVE COMMUNICATION　　227
    E. THE EXPERTISE OF THE CHOIR DIRECTOR　　230

ANSWERS TO EXERCISES　　　　　233

BIBLIOGRAPHY　　　　　　　　　247

GLOSSARY OF TERMS　　　　　　253

FOREWARD

To be called to lead, conduct, and rehearse – to gather together to be "the choir" – the voice of true worship of the Holy Church – how awesome and wonderful! By God's grace, be the leader you are called to be. Practice makes perfect.

Sacred singing gives voice to the words of our worship that teach, preach, and beseech, to gather together all who come in Christ's Name to celebrate the Holy Services of our Holy Church. The words we sing must be sung in a way that can be understood. This is the whole point of using English. But, without syntax and rhythm – phrasing – neither the music nor the text is truly understood.

Be careful to avoid the temptation to create "effects." Let the words sung as prayer sing for themselves! But, do work on the phrasing: the thought units, the stichs, the lines, the strophs, the movement of the words for rhythmic motion – the sound of worship, the voice of prayer.

God bless your sincere and noble efforts. God bless David Barrett for his wonderful textbook. Sing to the Lord!

Fr Sergei Glagolev
East Meadow, NY
June 2016

Fr Sergei Glagolev is a renowned music teacher and composer of Orthodox liturgical music.

PREFACE

Along with always seeming to have a shortage of priests available to serve our parishes, the Orthodox Church has also found it to be a fact that the available surplus of competent choir directors to serve in that ministry has also been very lean. In **both** cases (regarding clergy and choir directors), a major reason is that, in order to serve in these ministries, a serious period of study, hard work, and sacrificed time is needed to adequately prepare the person to function in these ministries. Concerning the situation with the training of choir directors, this problem has been addressed through the use of various local conducting classes in different deaneries and dioceses. Yet, a common complaint regarding these classes is that there is not sufficient material to use as an aid to supplement this training. This book attempts to address that need.

Very much of the material presented here was published in my first book, **Elementary Music Theory for Orthodox Liturgical Singing**.[1] **However**, there are **major** differences between the two books, based

---

[1] Barrett, David, *Elementary Music Theory for Orthodox Liturgical Singing*, OLP (Orthodox Liturgical Press), January 2014.

on the purpose of each. My first book was intended for **all** Church singers, both for those who do not know how to read music at all, and also for those who have a minimum knowledge and ability in this area. **This** book, by contrast, is intended **only** for the training of choir directors. Therefore, such basics as what a quarter note is, where middle **C** is on the staff, etc., need not be covered here. Since, though, a choir director needs to be able to intone the notes given to the various singers (what is colloquially known as "giving the pitch"), the skills required in mastering triadic harmony are essential! Furthermore, there are skills **not** needed by the average Church singer but that **are** required for a choir director, such as teaching the proper way to sing using diaphragmatic breathing, warm-up exercises, choir auditions and voice placing, rehearsal techniques (woodshedding, and so forth), etc. These skills, glossed over in the earlier book, will again be presented and expanded upon here.

    May God grant that those who are called into this joyful ministry of choir directing find this book to be an essential help in acquiring the skills to lead the people of God to worship, glorify, and give thanks to Him in joyful song and praise!

I. CONDUCTING ORTHODOX LITURGICAL MUSIC

1
SPIRITUAL AND LITURGICAL PREPARATION

There are many levels of preparation that a choir director needs to participate in before he or she can effectively function in this ministry. The major part of this book addresses the physiological, executional (singing), theoretical (music theory), directional (using the hands for beat patterns and expression), and preparatory (rehearsal) elements required to master the basic skills of conducting a choir. However, two additional, yet essentially vital, areas for a choir director are the need for spiritual and liturgical preparation.

A. SPIRITUAL PREPARATION

Since liturgical singing is a ***ministry***, that is, a participation in the two-natured aspect of the Church that, as the Body of Christ, is both divine and human, all Church singers and, especially, choir directors, must be communing Orthodox Christians who actively, consistently, and seriously participate in the life of the Church, as those who have been baptized to die and rise with Christ through living the sacramental life. This includes continuous participation in the Sacrament of Penance (Holy Confession), a regular, prayerful, and disciplined Communion in the Holy Eucharist, and participation in various other Sacraments, as called to (Holy Unction, Holy Matrimony, Holy Orders, etc.). As Leonid Ouspensky wrote in the book, ***The Meaning of Icons***:

> "In order to receive and pass on the testimony [of Holy Tradition], the iconographer must not only believe that it is genuine, but must also share in the life, by which the witness of the revelation lived, must follow the same way, that is, be a member of the body of the Church. Only then can he transmit the testimony received consciously and exactly. Hence the necessity for continual participation in the sacramental life of the Church; hence also the moral demands the Church makes of iconographers. For a true iconographer, creation is the way of asceticism and prayer,

that is, essentially, a monastic way. Although the beauty and content of an icon are perceived by each spectator subjectively, in accordance with his capacities, they are expressed by the iconographer objectively, through consciously surmounting his own 'I' and subjugating it to the revealed truth – the authority of the Tradition."[1]

This essential requirement for a serious participation in the life of the Church and the corresponding spiritual preparation on the part of the iconographer is the very same participation and preparation required of the Church musician, singer and director alike. Both iconography and Church singing are considered liturgical ministries, and, as such, require the same disciplines.

These spiritual disciplines result in clarity of mind, which is essential both in the spiritual life and in the task of fulfilling the various ministries of the Church. The following enumerates this clearly:

---

[1] Ouspensky, Leonid and Lossky, Vladimir, *The Meaning of Icons*, trans. G.E.H. Palmer and E. Kadloubovsky, SVS (St Vladimir's Seminary) Press, Crestwood, NY, 1982, p. 42.

"There are two means by which we can acquire such clarity of mind: the first and most necessary is prayer, by which we must implore the Holy Spirit to pour His divine light into our hearts. This He will surely do, if we truly seek God alone and sincerely strive to obey His will in everything, willingly submitting in all affairs to the advice of our experienced spiritual fathers and doing nothing without asking them.

The second method of exercising the mind is always to examine things and probe deep for knowledge of them, in order to see clearly which of them are good and which are bad. We should judge them not as the world and the senses do, but as they are judged by right season and the Holy Spirit, or by the word of the divinely-inspired Scriptures, or that of the holy fathers and teachers of the Church. For if this examination and deepening of knowledge is right and proper, it will quite certainly enable us to understand clearly that we must with all our heart regard as valueless, vain and false, all that the blind and depraved world loves and seeks."[1]

Silence, solitude, and stillness are necessary elements to "quiet" the self, in order to hear the "still, small voice" of God in the heart (1 Kg 19:12):

> "Our heart is, therefore, the shrine of the intelligence and the chief intellectual organ of the body. When, therefore, we strive to scrutinize and to amend our intelligence through rigorous watchfulness, how could we do this if we did not collect our intellect, outwardly dispersed through the senses, and bring it back within ourselves – back to the heart itself, the shrine of the thoughts? It is for this reason that St Makarios – rightly called blessed – directly after what he says above,

---

[1] *Unseen Warfare, the Spiritual Combat and Path to Paradise of Lorenzo Scupoli*, edited by Nicodemus of the Holy Mountain and revised by Theophan the Recluse, translated by E. Kadloubovsky and G.E.H. Palmer, introduction by H.A. Hodges, M.A., D.Phil, Professor of Philosophy, SVS Press, Crestwood, NY, 1978, p. 90.

ads: 'So it is there that we must look to see whether grace has inscribed the laws of the Spirit.' Where? In the ruling organ, in the throne of grace, where the intellect and all the thoughts of the soul reside, that is to say, in the heart. Do you see, then, how greatly necessary it is for those who have chosen a life of self-attentiveness and stillness to bring their intellect back and to enclose it within their body, and particularly within that innermost body within the body that we call the heart?"[2]

At the St Sergius Orthodox Institute in Paris in 1997, Dr Dimitri Conomos gave a lecture entitled, "Early Christian and Byzantine Music: History and Performance". In the second section, which he called "Liturgical Music and Orthodox Spirituality",

---

[2] St Gregory Palamas, "In Defense of Those who Devoutly Practice a Life of Stillness", *The Philokalia: The Complete Text, Volume IV*, compiled by St Nikodemos of the Holy Mountain and St Makarios of Corinth, translated from the Greek and edited by G.E.H. Palmer, Philip Sherrard, Kallistos Ware, with the assistance of the Holy Transfiguration Monastery (Brookline), Constantine Cavarnos, Dana Miller, Basil Osborne, and Norman Russell, Faber and Faber, London, England, 1995, p. 334.

Spiritual and Liturgical Preparation

Dr Conomos cited three fundamental concepts in Orthodox spirituality that can be made to apply to our Church music. These are the following (these sections are direct quotes from his lecture):

1. **Asceticism** is the call for self-denial, self-dissatisfaction; and the constant yearning for improvement through hard work and energetic application….The Church singer has a sacred profession, and this sanctity requires a determination of character, a strong faith, great modesty, and a high sense of integrity. To be a Church singer in an Orthodox Church is to respond to a calling, to a vocation – it demands purity, sureness of faith, and conviction.

2. **Holiness**. And what is meant by the **holiness** of our vocation?...Holiness means otherness, sacredness, apartness – not the common or the ordinary, but the unique, the particular, the uncontaminated.

3. **Apatheia, or "passionlessness"**….This idea of passionlessness is perhaps most reflected in the best Orthodox iconography – where the saint is painted

in colours and shapes that transcend everything that is fleshly, sensual, and cosmetic.

These truths are so ontological that they are beginning to be recognized even in the secular world. James Jordan, in his textbook, **Evoking Sounds**, says the following:

> "Access can only be gained through quiet and stillness within oneself. Quiet solitude must be a daily occurrence. Stillness is a deliberate choice. You must consciously choose stillness. Unfortunately, the world will not give it to you. Additionally, you must choose stillness over and over again in very difficult situations when it might be easier not to choose stillness. Initially, the discovery of stillness within oneself brings great joy. Soon, however, it brings difficulties and darkness. You will discover that the newfound stillness unmakes personality so you can become a person. By being still, you are able to make

yourself less allows the music to speak clearly through the ensemble."[3]

This process of "making ourselves less so others can become more" is reminiscent of the words of St John the Baptist (whom our Lord said was the greatest born of woman), when he said, "He [Christ] must increase, but I must decrease" (Jn 3:30). Through this process, we surrender our entire selves, our egos, our preconceptions, our prejudices, our tastes, likes, and dislikes, to God, so that everything that we do in this ministry of Orthodox liturgical music is for **His** glory, and **not** for ours. The demons of individualism, selfishness, pride, and jealously must be rooted out, and, as our Lord has said, "This kind never comes out except by prayer and fasting!" (Mt 17:31; Mk 9:29). It is easy to become self-centered to the point of making the music an end in itself. For example, even though the Typikon specifies a certain number of stikhera for

---

[3] Jordan, James, *Evoking Sound: Fundamentals of Choral Conducting*, Second Edition, Foreword by Morten Lauridsen, with chapters by Robert W. Rumbelow and James Whitbourn, GIA Publications, Inc., Chicago, IL, 2009 (hereafter referred to as "*Evoking Sound*"), p. 18.

the day and the saints on "Lord, I Call Upon You," many parish priests, for the pastoral purpose of keeping the length of Vespers to a comfortable level for his parishioners, will limit the singing of stikhera for the saints to only those who are considered major saints, like, St Sergius of Radonezh. However, there those choir directors who eagerly try to talk their pastors into doing all the stikhera called for in the Typikon, even for minor saints whom nobody in the parish has heard of. Surrendering ourselves to God to serve **Him** in **His** Church ("**Your** will be done, on Earth as it is in Heaven!") ensures that things are done "decently and in order" (1 Cor 14:40) in the balanced perspective of humble service in the ministry of Orthodox liturgical music.

B. LITURGICAL PREPARATION

Another vital but often-overlooked area of preparation for choir directors is that of liturgical preparation. There are many directors who have great difficulty in their ministry because they do not know the order of the services beyond the Saturday evening Great Vespers and the Sunday morning Divine Liturgy. Services such as Vigil, Presanctified Liturgy, Funeral, Wedding, Compline, and the services of Holy Week and Pascha cause some directors great anxiety, confusion, and frustration. There are various service books of the Church that can be referred to in order to clarify the order of each particular service.[4] There are also books that give a general outline of the services with the specifics of how they differ in each of the various practices (Russian, Greek, Antiochian, etc.).[5] Finally, ***all*** choir directors should sit down and go over the services with their parish priest beforehand.

Even more essential for every choir director to realize is that liturgical music is ontologically (that is, by its very being) just that: ***liturgical***! As Mark Bailey pointed out:

---

[4] A complete list of these service books is provided in the Bibliography at the end of this book.
[5] Cf. Barrett, David, *Liturgics for Orthodox Liturgical Singing, Volume 1* (July 2014) and *Volume 2* (January 2015), OLP (Orthodox Liturgical Press), Southbury, CT.

By principle, liturgy is not an element of music, however important and even essential musicological study may deem that element to be, but music is an element of liturgy. In other words, worship is the raison d'Ltre of the (C)hurch, and worship therefore serves as the point of departure and the point of arrival that should necessarily frame the entire process of musical examination.[6]

This awareness and perspective is not only a necessary prerequisite for all Church musicians (especially choir directors) but also a **primary factor** in their ministry:

To start, the (C)hurch's liturgy or patterns of worship are the primary subjects for examination. In other words, liturgical musicians should seek broadly and in detail to understand the liturgical structures, systems, and points of emphasis that specifically formulate and guide worship in the missionary

---

[6] Bailey, Mark, "Toward a Living Tradition of Liturgical Music in North America", *St Vladimir's Theological Quarterly*, Volume 47, Number 2, 2003, p. 192.

(C)hurch, and to respond to this understanding with the appropriate musical expression of those elements. Musicians must also take into account the more general inclinations and manifestations of the gathered faithful in response to their communal unity in such a (C)hurch.[7]

    The order of the words in the descriptive title of "liturgical music" is thus important: It is the *liturgical* element or component that comes first and is *primary*, and *then* the musical element or component. That is, the musical element is secondary and *subservient* to the liturgical element, which gives the musical element its *only* reason for being. Otherwise, so-called "liturgical music" just ends up being secular music with a religious subject matter that is "performed" in services, rather than being the component that makes the *worship* in liturgy come alive.[8] Without this vitally essential realization and perspective on the part of Church musicians, the choir director will come to view the music of liturgy as an end in itself, divorced from its

---

[7] *Ibid*, p. 196.
[8] *Ibid*, p. 193.

sole and ***primary function*** of giving shape to, enhancing, and manifesting the functions of the liturgical rites. Then, there will be more attention given to the choice of which musical arrangements of a hymn will be sung, based on musical taste and aesthetics rather than on how the setting appropriately reveals the function of the liturgical action the hymn is paired with. This essential component of liturgical preparation is even more lacking on the part of our liturgical musicians nowadays than the spiritual preparation is. It is ***crucial*** that ***all*** choir directors spend a ***great*** deal of time and study in acquiring an authentically Orthodox liturgical perspective, deeply internalizing the fact of the primacy of the liturgical component over the musical one, and examining and evaluating all musical elements, choices, and decisions in deference to the liturgical elements and their functions within the services themselves.

2
POSTURE, BREATHING, AND TONE PLACEMENT

As a director, if you are going to instruct and train your choir members to sing properly, three essential areas you will need to work on in your teaching is in maintaining correct posture, the proper method of breathing, and tone placement. All of these elements are essential in order to sing in an appropriate manner to the glory of God.

A. POSTURE

Correct posture and body alignment are crucial for quality singing. A person who exhibits poor posture, with their inner entrails misaligned and pressing together, cannot possibly manifest proper breath support and execute tones of quality and beauty. Good posture places the bodily organs in their appropriate position and ensures maximum strength and support for tone production of the highest order.

Concerning posture, the best and simplest concept to remember is "***back*** and ***down***": that is, the shoulders should be pulled back into a ***comfortable*** position (not so far back that the muscles are straining) and down, also to a point of natural comfortability. A posture that is forward and down leads to the round-shouldered position of bad posture (like a person with osteoporosis), and a posture that is back and up, with the shoulders touching the ears, leads to a position of stiffness and rigidity (like the Frankenstein monster in the movies). A posture that keeps the shoulders back and down, naturally and comfortably, ensures the best positioning of the body. Along with this, singers and choir directors may want to pursue ways to align the body to its most natural and supportive position.[1]

B. BREATHING

The second essential element required for quality singing is that of proper breathing and breath support. Most people breathe in a shallow manner,

---

[1] For a detailed presentation of proper body alignment, cf. *Evoking Sound*, pp. 25-39.

utilizing only their lungs. This may suffice for routine activity and a sedentary lifestyle, but it is totally inadequate for the task of choral music production.

The way to good breathing and breath support is to embrace your "DIB's": DIB, or Diaphragmatic Intercostal Breathing, is the practice of breathing throughout the entire cavity comprising the respiratory and digestive tracts. It consists of contracting the diaphragm, a muscle located horizontally between the chest cavity and the stomach cavity.[2]

The easiest way to learn and master the art of DIB is to either stand straight against a flat wall or, better yet, to lie down on your back on a floor or bed with firm back support. Placing your hand on your lower stomach area (right below the navel), take in a deep breath slowly while **simultaneously** pushing your hand out and up with your stomach. Think of it as similar to using a bellows for a fireplace or an accordion: as air enters, the bellows or accordion expands to let the maximum amount of air enter and fill up the unit. The same concept works with your body: as you breathe in while, at the same time, expanding your stomach up and out, you end up drawing air not only into your lungs but into your

---

[2] Internet site, Wikipedia, under "Diaphragmatic Breathing."

entire diaphragm and stomach cavity. Suddenly taking in this much higher quantity of air can initially result in lightheadedness, which is why it is recommended to begin this exercising lying down, rather than standing up. With regular and consisted practice, the body will naturally adjust to this new level of maximum air input, and the lightheadedness will quickly dissipate.

    A healthy and humble way to begin is to lie down and practice this breathing for five minutes a day for the first week or two. During this time, just breathe deeply into your lower diaphragmatic area in a natural manner, neither forcing the air in or out, nor trying to hold your breath or the air in this lower cavity. After two or three weeks of practicing this, at which time the lightheadedness should dissipate, then, beginning with the fourth or fifth week, practice breathing naturally like this for five minutes, followed by five minutes of breathing in deeply, holding the breath in the lower diaphragmatic area for a few ***comfortable*** seconds, and then slowly releasing it. Again, a gradual buildup of this skill is essential. There is no need to try to become a "respiratory body-builder", and doing this exercise on a level of comfortability will ensure that no muscles are unnecessarily pulled or strained. After a week or two of this, continue the regular breathing cycle for the first five minutes and, in the second five minutes of holding the breath, try to increase the breath holding time by only a second or two. This is parallel to gradual bodybuilding: by increasing the held breath slowly and incrementally, you will consistently and **safely** build up the diaphragm muscles to a level of strength and support.

You will then discover it to be **much** easier to maintain a quality tone while singing, coupled with consistent pitch retention (many singers go "flat" in singing their notes because of improper breathing and poor breath support) and more successful sustained singing of longer notes in the hymns. This, in turn, leads to better phrasing in the liturgical singing (text phrases thereby don't end up chopped and fragmented), whereby the context of the liturgical hymns is better understood and more easily prayed with on the part of the congregation. When you have successfully mastered this skill, you can then, in turn, take some quality rehearsal time to teach it to your choir singers, as well.

C. TONE PLACEMENT

Tone placement is literally what it sounds like: placing the tone in the head, the point of placement depending on the tone's pitch, volume, and length of sound. One way to think of the human body is to use the image of the "shepherd's hook": a side view of the body would show the nasal cavity, the roundness of the head, and then the vertical aspect of the rest of the body. This is illustrated below.

Example 1

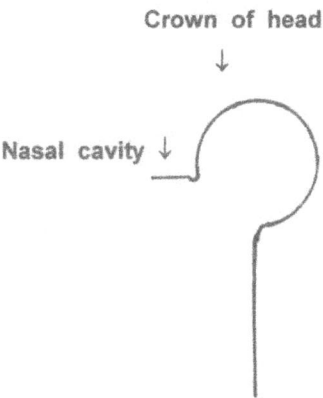

Spiritual and Liturgical Preparation 23

When a person sings a tone in the lower, more comfortable area of their pitch range (all the tones that they are able to sing, from lowest to highest), at a medium volume and for a short duration of time, that tone can be "placed" in the nasal cavity, in the middle area of the nose (considered vertically) and in front (considered horizontally). As this person sings up a scale or upwards in their pitch range, to higher tones, these subsequent tones need to be "placed" higher up in the nasal cavity, until, reaching the very highest tones in their range, the person would "place" the tone in the crown of the head. Likewise, for tones that require an increase in volume and/or duration, these tones would need to be "placed" higher in the nasal cavity, as well.

What does it mean, exactly, to "place" a tone? Simply put, it means projecting the tone to a specific place in the nasal cavity through imagining the tone already being in that specific place. So, for example, a woman singing soprano would sing a high-pitched tone by imagining that this tone is in the crown of her head. In other words, she would use her mind to project the tone upwards and "place" it in the crown of her head. The human mind and imagination are very powerful. Scientific studies have proven that people can, with training, actually control the functioning of their bodies through mental effort (regulating pulse and/or blood pressure, lowering body temperature, etc.). With regular, sustained, and patient practice, singers can gradually master the skill of placing tones at the various levels of the nasal and head cavities, based on the requirements of pitch, volume, and tone duration.[3] This skill, coupled with appropriate posture and Diaphragmatic Intercostal Breathing and breath support, will ensure the highest quality of tone production and singing on the part of choir members.

EXERCISES • CHAPTER 2

1. Standing in front of a full-length mirror, practice forming good posture by bringing the shoulders comfortably back and down. Hold your

---

[3] What I have referred to here as "tone placement" has been called "breath placement" or "air flow placement" by others who are expert at teaching proper singing techniques. Cf., especially, Holwey, Phil, *So You Want to Sing?*, Illustrations by Nancy Potts, Cover by Kathie Holwey, self-published by Philip L. Holwey, 1977, pp. 10-15 and 39-41 (available on Amazon.com). This is an *excellent* guide and textbook, fully illustrated, on the rudiments of posture, breathing, and tone placement.

body in this position in a relaxed manner (not stiffening or tightening the muscles of your body, especially the head, neck, and shoulders). Stand comfortably in this position for about five minutes a day, each day, for two weeks. Then, increase the time to ten minutes each day for another two weeks. At the end of this period, this new correct posture should have become a part of you. If, at any time, you find yourself slipping into your old inappropriate posture, return to this exercise until your body "remembers" the new posture on its own.

You can also use this exercise in your choir rehearsals. Have everyone assume the correct "back-and-down" posture of the shoulders, and, once achieved, have everyone maintain this for five minutes. Instruct your singers to practice this in front of a full-length mirror at home for five minutes a day, as their "homework assignment."

2. Lying flat on your back on the floor or on a bed with good back support, place your hand on your stomach below the navel and breathe in slowly while **simultaneously** using your stomach to push your hand up and out. Practice this for five minutes a day, each day, for three or four weeks. Then, each

day, practice this breathing exercise for five minutes, followed by another five minutes of breathing in using this correct technique, holding the breath briefly, and then letting it out slowly.

Again, this exercise can also be taught to your singers at your choir rehearsal. Here, instead of having everyone lie down, you can have them stand with their backs flat against the wall. Demonstrate to them how to breathe using their diaphragm (remember, having the hand flat on the stomach and pushing it up and out while breathing in is essential), then have everyone in the choir try it. As their "homework assignment" for this skill, instruct them how to do this at home, telling them to lie flat on the floor or the bed (again, remember that, at first, taking in this larger quantity of air will result in a temporary lightheadedness). In subsequent rehearsals over the next month or so, spend the first five minutes of the rehearsal practicing the DIB with the hand placement on the stomach. In short order, you will find your singers breathing properly and sustaining better tone production.

3. Begin singing tones starting in your low comfortable range, using a neutral syllable like "lu". Do this entire exercise with your eyes closed. Place

Spiritual and Liturgical Preparation 27

the first of these tones in your lower nasal cavity (midpoint in the nose vertically, out to the front horizontally). As you sing up a scale and/or your pitch range, gradually place the tones higher as needed until, with the upper tones of your pitch range, the tones are placed in the crown of the head.

At your choir rehearsal, demonstrate this exercise for your singers. Then, have them close their eyes for the exercise. Explain that, as they do this exercise with you and move up the scale, they will have to place the tones higher in their nasal cavities the higher they go in pitch. Sing a lower comfortable tone on "lu". Have your singers repeat it. After they do this, move up the scale by half-step to the next tone and sing it on "lu". Have your singers repeat it. Do this repeatedly, going up the scale by half-steps. When you get to the top, repeat the top note, then reverse direction, coming down the scale by half-steps until you reach the lowest tone again. Once this exercise has been taught to your choir, practice it for five minutes at the beginning of a rehearsal once a month. Eventually, your singers will naturally master the skill of tone placement.

3
TRIADIC HARMONY

The *first* thing a choir director does at the beginning of a service is to what is colloquially known as "giving the pitch". For example, when the main celebrant chants the doxology of the service ("Blessed is our God,…!", "Glory to the holy, consubstantial,…!", or "Blessed is the Kingdom…!"), the choir director has to intone the notes that each section of the choir (usually, soprano, alto, tenor, and bass) will sing and, furthermore, to give those notes in their proper order. ***Therefore***, a knowledge of triadic harmony is ***essential***.[1] Even choir directors in the Byzantine tradition, where triadic harmony is replaced by Byzantine chant that utilizes a melody and an ison, need to understand triadic harmony because, many times, the melody and ison begin on

---

[1] Some of the material presented here and in subsequent chapters was covered in my book, *Elementary Music Theory for Orthodox Liturgical Singing*, OLP (Orthodox Liturgical Press), January 2014. For the sake of thoroughness, and to preclude the need for readers to have to purchase this other book, that same material will be duplicated and expanded upon here, in *this* book.

different notes, notes which have a relationship to one another (the root and the fifth of a chord, for example) that have a basis in triadic harmony.

A. MAJOR SCALES

Beginning at middle **C** on your keyboard, play all of the white keys up to the next **C**, and then down the same white keys to middle **C** again.

Example 2

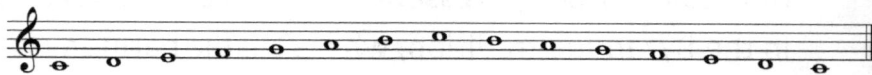

This is the **C** major scale. A *scale* is a series of ascending and descending tones arranged in a pattern.[2] It is the particular pattern used which will determine what type of scale it is. Examining this *C* major scale, we can discover where the whole steps and half steps occur in the scale. Applying this pattern to the *C* major scale, the whole steps and half steps occur as follows.

Example 3

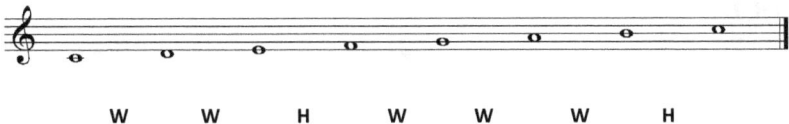

Between *C* and *D*, there is a whole step. This is also the case from *D* to *E*. From *E* to *F*, however, there is a half step. A whole step then occurs again from *F* to *G*, *G* to *A*, and *A* to *B*. From *B* to *C*, though, there is a half step. Thus, the pattern of whole steps and half

---

[2]Christ, William; DeLone, Richard; Kliewer, Vernon; Rowell, Lewis; and Thomson, William; *Materials and Structure of Music, Volume 1*, 2nd Edition, Prentice-Hall, Inc., Englewood Cliffs, NJ, 1972 (hereafter referred to as "*Materials*"), p. 1.

steps for a *major* scale is: **W**hole, **W**hole, **H**alf, **W**hole, **W**hole, **W**hole, **H**alf; or ***W*, *W*, *H*, *W*, *W*, *W*, *H*.**[3] It is this particular arrangement of whole steps and half steps which gives a major scale its quality of being "major".

Double-check the pattern of whole steps and half steps for a major scale by examining the ***F*** major scale. This scale has one flat: ***B*^{b}**. Play up the keyboard, beginning on the ***F*** above middle ***C***, remembering to play the black key just to the left of ***B*** for ***B*^{b}**.

Example 4

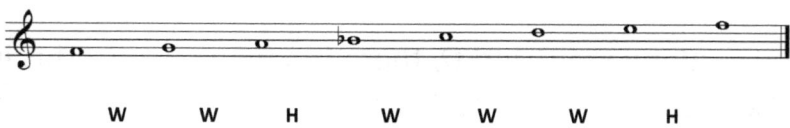

Examining the ***F*** major scale, a whole step is found between ***F*** and ***G***, and again between ***G*** and ***A***. However, between ***A*** and ***B***, a whole step occurs, at a

---

[3]Ibid, p. 39.

point in the scale pattern where a half step is called for. By lowering the **B** to **B^b** (as in Example 27 above), the interval is reduced from a whole step to a half step. The next part of the pattern calls for a whole step. Between **B** and **C**, there is a half step. But, since the **B** was lowered to **B^b**, the half step is increased to a whole step: a half step between **B^b** and **B** , and another half step between **B** and **C**. Therefore, **B^b** to **C** is a whole step, as is **C** to **D**, and **D** to **E**. **E** to **F** is a half step, which is what the pattern for a major scale calls for here. So, the **F** major scale, **with its B^b**, satisfies the pattern for a major scale of **W, W, H, W, W, W, H**. Play the **F** major scale again on your keyboard. The **pattern** of notes sounds the same as that for the **C** major scale, because the pattern of whole steps and half steps is the same.

B. SCALE DEGREES

Play again the **C** major scale ascending.

Example 5

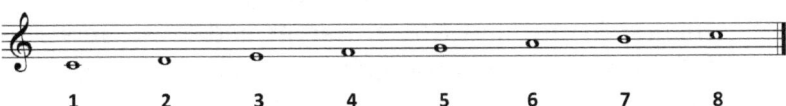

1 2 3 4 5 6 7 8

The numbers under the notes of the scale refer to **scale degrees**, which classify the particular functions of the notes within the scale.[4] Thus, in the **C** major scale, **C** is the 1st degree of the scale, **D** is the 2nd degree, **E** is the 3rd degree, etc. When the 8th degree of the scale is reached, it is at the octave of the 1st degree (in this example, **C**).

Technical names are given to the scale degrees to describe their function within the scale:[5]

1. **Tonic**: the "home tone" or tone of focus of the scale.
2. **Supertonic:** the next tone above the tonic.
3. **Mediant:** the tone halfway between the tonic and its dominant (halfway between 1 and 5).
4. **Sub-Dominant:** the tone a fourth above or a fifth below (the "under dominant") the tonic.
5. **Dominant:** the tone a fifth above the tonic.

---

[4]Ibid, p. 41. Cf, also, Jones, George Thaddeus, *Music Theory*, Barnes and Noble, Harper and Row, New York, NY, 1974 (hereafter referred to as "*Theory*"), p. 60.
[5]Ibid.

6   **Sub-Mediant:** the tone halfway between the sub-dominant and the tonic (halfway between 6 and 8).
7   **Leading Tone**: the tone a ***half*** step below the tonic, which leads up to it. When it is a ***whole*** step below the tonic, it is called the **Sub-Tonic**.
8   **Tonic**: the octave of the tonic at scale degree 1.

C. KEYS AND KEY SIGNATURES

A ***key*** is the name given to the tonal center of a scale or musical composition.[6] Thus, the note ***C*** is the tonal center of the key of ***C*** major, ***G*** is the tonal center of the key of ***G*** major, etc. The designation of the key tells us which note is the tonic, the "home tone", to which all the other notes refer. There are twelve notes in the Western musical system from which keys are formed and scales are built: ***A, A#** (B^b)*, ***B, C, C#** (D^b)**, D, D#** (E^b)**, E, F, F#** (G^b)**, G**, and ***G#** (A^b)*.

---

[6]*Materials*, p. 34f. Cf., *Theory*, p. 40f.

If a musical composition is in the key of **F** major, which has **B**^{b}, it is much clearer to write this one flat at the beginning of the staff than to write it before each and every **B**. The set of sharps or flats, or the lack of them, at the beginning of a musical line or composition is called a ***key signature***.[7]

Example 6

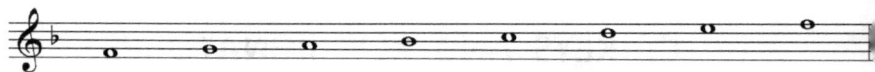

The key signature gives the music a cleaner look that is easier to read.

The following are the key signatures for all of the flat keys that are major.[8]

---

[7] *Materials*, pp. 42-46. Cf., *Theory*, p. 34f.
[8] *Theory*, p. 35.

Example 7

The following are the key signatures for all of the sharp keys that are major.[9]

Example 8

The key signature of **C** major has **no** sharps or flats. Since our liturgical music does not use any musical instrument except the human voice, it is unlikely that you will find much of it with key

---

[9]Ibid.

signatures beyond three or four sharps or flats. The complete group of the key signatures is presented here for reference.

D. SOLFEGE SYLLABLES

One of the most widely used systems for reading scale degrees within keys makes use of a series of syllables where one syllable is assigned to each scale degree. These syllables are known as ***solfege syllables***, and the system for using these is called the ***solfege system***.[10] The solfege syllables are ***Do***, ***Re***, ***Mi***, ***Fa***, ***Sol***, ***La***, ***Ti***, and (again) ***Do***.

There are two variations of the solfege system. One is called the Fixed ***Do*** System, where a syllable is assigned to each ***note*** (such as ***C***, ***D***, ***E***, etc.). The other one, the Movable ***Do*** System, assigns a syllable to each ***scale degree*** and, therefore, establishes a ***relationship*** between the solfege syllable and the ***function*** of the scale degree within a given key. This Movable ***Do*** System is the one most prevalent in the

---

[10]*Harvard*, pp. 785-786, under "Solfege, solfeggio". Cf., *Theory*, p. 22.

United States, and the one that will be presented here.

Play the *C* major scale again on your keyboard, and sing it using the solfege syllables in the example below.

Example 9

Since there is a half step between *E* and *F*, and again between *B* and *C*, the half steps in the Movable *Do* System *always* fall between the syllables *Mi* and *Fa* and between *Ti* and *Do*. Verify this by singing the solfege syllables in the example below while playing the *F* major scale on your keyboard, playing the black key for B^b.

Example 10

Between **Mi** and **Fa**, there is a half step between **A** and **B**^{b}. There is also a half step between **Ti** and **Do** with the notes **E** to **F**.

E. MINOR KEYS AND SCALES

In the Western harmonic system, keys and scales can be major or minor. One way to remember minor scales is in relation to major scales.[11] Remembering that the tonic is the "home tone" of a key, the tonic of the key of **C** major is the note **C**, which is **Do** in the solfege pattern for a major scale.

---

[11]*Materials*, p. 43.

Example 11

Backing up two notes, a scale can be constructed with no sharps or flats on the note **A**.

Example 12

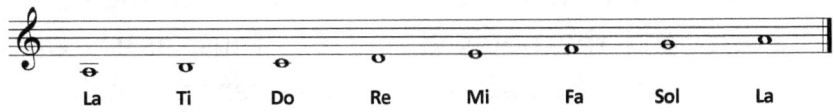

This is an example of a ***minor scale***. When referring to major scales, capital letters are used (**C** major); minor scales are designated by lower case letters (***a*** minor). Since **C** major and ***a*** minor share the same key signature (no sharps or flats), *a* minor is the ***relative minor*** of ***C*** major.[12]

The following example illustrates the pattern of whole steps and half steps for a minor scale.

Example 13

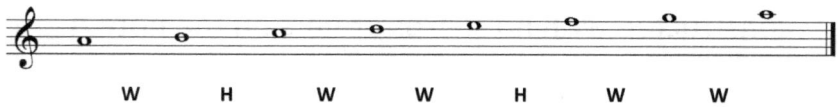

Between the "white key" notes of the keyboard there are all whole steps, except between the notes ***E*** and ***F*** and the notes ***B*** and ***C***. Thus, as shown in Example 36, the pattern of whole steps and half steps for a ***minor*** scale is: ***W***hole, ***H***alf, ***W***hole, ***W***hole, ***H***alf, ***W***hole, ***W***hole, or ***W, H, W, W, H, W, W***.[13] Again, it is this particular arrangement of whole steps and half steps which gives this scale the quality of being "minor".

---

[12] Ibid.

[13] *Theory*, p. 33.

The ***a*** minor scale was constructed by going back two notes from its relative major, ***C*** major. Therefore, while the tonic or "home tone" of a ***major*** key is ***Do***, the tonic for a ***minor*** key is ***La***. Applying this to all of the minor scales, all minor key signatures can be constructed. The following are the key signatures for all of the flat keys that are minor.[14]

Example 14

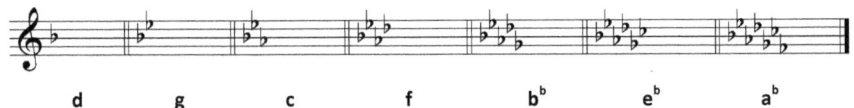

The following are the key signatures for all of the sharp keys that are minor.[15]

Example 15

---

[14]Ibid, p. 35.
[15]Ibid.

Again, occurrences of minor key signatures of more than three or four sharps or flats in our liturgical music will be rare.

F. CHORDS AND TRIADS

Play the **C** major scale on your keyboard, beginning on middle **C**.

Example 16

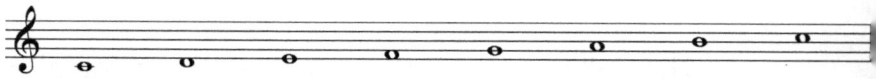

Now play a set of four alternating notes on top of each note of the scale.

Example 17

Triadic Harmony

These groupings of notes are called chords. A ***chord*** is a group of three or more alternate pitches, sounding simultaneously.[16] Building chords of only three alternate pitches on the scale tones results in the following.

Example 18

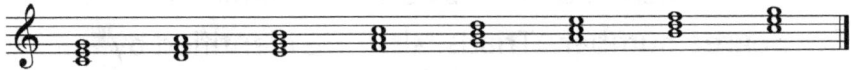

This type of chord is called a triad. A ***triad*** is a chord of three alternate pitches, consisting of a root, a 3rd, and a 5th.[17] In the first triad of example 41, it begins on middle ***C***, skips over ***D*** to go to ***E***, then skips over ***F*** to go to ***G***. The first triad, then, is comprised of ***C***, ***E***, and ***G***. The second triad is made up of ***D***, ***F***, and ***A***; the third triad consists of ***E***, ***G***, and ***B***; etc.

---

[16]*Theory*, p. 49f. Cf., *Materials*, p. 206f.
[17]*Theory*, pp. 52-53. Cf., *Materials*, pp. 28-29.

The **root** is the basic tone of a chord or triad.[18] It is the tone on which other chord tones are built. In the first triad above, **C** is the root of the triad. Since **E** is a 3rd above the **C** (**C**, **D**, **E**) and **G** is a 5th above the **C**, **E** is the **3rd** of the triad and **G** is the **5th** of the triad. Looking at the next triad, **D** is the root, **F** is the 3rd, and **A** is the 5th. In the third triad, **E** is the root, **G** is the 3rd, and **B** is the 5th. The same analysis can be made with the remaining triads.

Each note of a scale can be named by a scale degree number. Triads, also, are identified by numbers, most often by Roman numerals.

Example 19

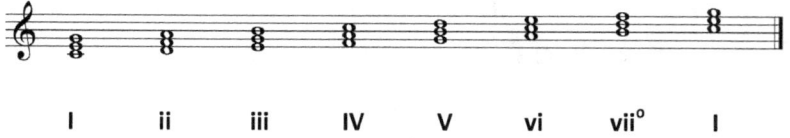

   I   ii   iii   IV   V   vi   vii°   I

---

[18]*Theory*, p. 50. Cf., *Materials*, p. 25f.

The first triad in this example, made up of **C**, **E**, and **G**, is the first chord in the key of **C** major. Since it is built on the 1st degree of the scale (**C**), it is called the "I chord" ("one chord") in the key of **C** major. The triad built on the second degree of the **C** major scale (**D**) is called the ii chord; the triad built on the third degree of the **C** major scale (**E**) is called the iii chord; etc.

Play each triad of the **C** major scale again, starting with the I chord. Play up and down the scale on each triad a few times. Become familiar with how the triads differ in quality of sound from each other.

G. QUALITIES OF INTERVALS AND TRIADS

The quality of an interval is determined by how many half steps the top note of the interval is over the bottom note. When abbreviating interval designations, "M" is used for "major", "m" designates "minor", "P" means "perfect", "º" indicates "diminished", and "+" means "augmented".[19] Using these designations, the following example illustrates

---

[19]*Materials*, p. 17.

how many half steps are found in each type of interval within an octave.

Example 20

Unison	0 half steps	**m2**	1 half step
M2	2 half steps	**m3**	3 half steps
M3	4 half steps	**P4**	5 half steps
°5 (+4)	6 half steps	**P5**	7 half steps
m6	8 half steps	**M6**	9 half steps
m7	10 half steps	**M7**	11 half steps
octave	12 half steps		

An ***augmented interval*** is one half step larger than a major or perfect interval, while a ***diminished interval*** is one half step smaller than a minor or perfect interval; a ***perfect interval*** refers only to unisons, 4ths, 5ths, and octaves.[20]

Interval sizes can be verified by referring to the illustration of the musical keyboard.

---

[20]Ibid.

Example 21

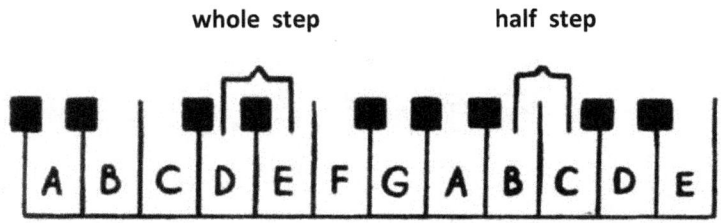

C to E is a major 3rd that, according to example 43, is four half steps. The keyboard illustration verifies this, since C to $C^{\#}$ (D^b) is one half step, $C^{\#}$ (D^b) to D is a second half step, D to $D^{\#}$ (E^b) is a third half step, and $D^{\#}$ (E^b) to E is the fourth half step. The keyboard can be used to verify all other intervals illustrated in example 43.

How is this information concerning interval sizes useful for our knowledge of triads? It is the combination of various types of intervals that determines the quality of a triad. There are actually three intervals within a triad.[21]

---

[21]*Theory*, p. 53.

Example 22

There is a 3rd from the root of the triad to the 3rd (in this case, **C** to **E**); there is a 3rd from the 3rd of the triad to the 5th (here, **E** to **G**); and there is a 5th from the root of the triad to the 5th (**C** to **G** in this example). Examining the number of half steps involved, it is shown that **C** to **E** is a M3 (major 3rd), **E** to **G** is a m3 (minor 3rd), and **C** to **G** is a P5 (perfect 5th).

Example 23

Triadic Harmony

This is a ***major triad***, which consists of a major 3rd, a minor 3rd, and a perfect 5th.[22] For reference, many major triads that you may encounter are given below.

Example 24

A ***minor triad*** consists of a minor 3rd, a major 3rd, and a perfect 5th.[23]

---

[22] Ibid.
[23] Ibid.

Example 25

The only difference between major and minor triads is the arrangement of the 3rds. The major triad has a major 3rd, then a minor 3rd; the minor triad has a minor 3rd, then a major 3rd. Both types of triads have perfect 5ths. For reference, many minor triads that you may encounter are given below.

Example 26

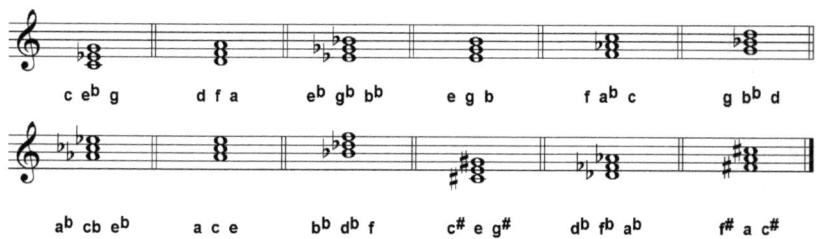

Another way of looking at qualities of intervals and triads is by examining the relationship between the tones of an interval or triad within the given key of the root note. For example, it can be said that C to E is a major 3rd because, ***in the key of C major***, E is natural. Likewise, it can be stated that C to E^b is a minor 3rd because, ***in the key of c minor***, the E is flatted (E^b). Therefore, a knowledge of key signatures can aid in qualifying intervals and triads.

H. 7TH CHORDS

The triad consists of three alternate pitches, a root, a 3rd, and a 5th. If one more alternate pitch is stacked onto the triad, the result is a 7th chord. A ***7th chord*** consists of four alternate pitches: a root, a 3rd, a 5th, and a 7th.[24] This last note is called a 7th because it is at the interval of a 7th above the root of the chord.

---

[24]*Theory*, pp. 53-55. Cf., *Materials*, p. 313f.

Example 27

The 7th on top of the 7th chord in this example is ***B^b***. Since *B* occurs as ***B natural*** in the key of ***C*** major, ***C*** to ***B^b*** is a minor 7th. This form of the 7th chord, with the minor 7th, is common in music, especially when built on the V chord.

I. INVERSIONS

It is important for choir directors and singers to know what position a triad is in. This has to do with the note in the bass, which is the lowest voice. This bass functions as a foundation for the triad. This foundation is strongest when the root of the triad is in the lowest voice.

Example 28

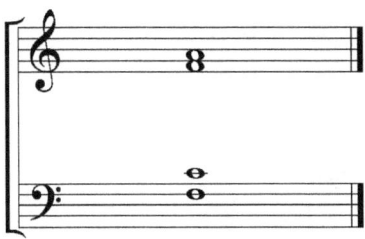

When a triad is built with the root in the lowest voice, the triad is in ***root position***.[25] Reading the triad in this example from the bottom up, the **F** major triad has the root on **F** in the bass line, the 5th on **C** in the tenor line, the root on **F** duplicated in the alto line, and the 3rd on **A** in the soprano line. Play this arrangement on your keyboard.

An ***inversion*** is a redistribution of chord tones out of root position.[26] Replacing the bottom **F** of the triad with **A** will result in the 3rd of the triad being in the lowest voice. Play the following triad arrangement on your keyboard.

---

[25]*Theory*, pp. 52-53. Cf., *Materials*, pp. 224-228.
[26]Ibid.

Example 29

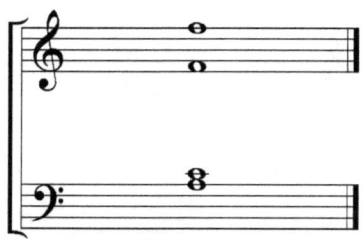

When a triad has the 3rd of the chord in the bass, it is in *first inversion*.

Replacing the **A** in the bass line with the **C** results in the 5th of the triad being in the lowest voice. Play this arrangement of the triad on your keyboard.

Example 30

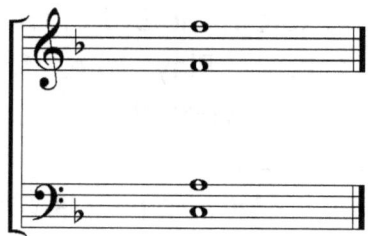

When a triad has the 5th of the chord in the bass, it is in *second inversion*.

The final substitution involves the 7th chord. Play the following arrangement of the 7th chord on your keyboard, with *E^b* in the bass voice, *C* in the tenor, *F* in the alto, and *A* in the soprano.

Example 31

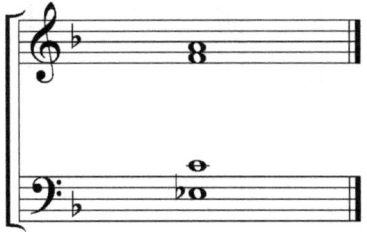

When a 7th chord has the 7th in the bass, it is in *third inversion*. Play examples 51 through 54 again. Notice that, as the bass note continually gets further away from the root of the chord (first the 3rd, then the 5th, then the 7th), the feeling for the root of the chord becomes weaker.

J. TRIADS IN MAJOR AND MINOR KEYS

The following example illustrates the triads of the key of *C* major. Play these on your keyboard.

Example 32

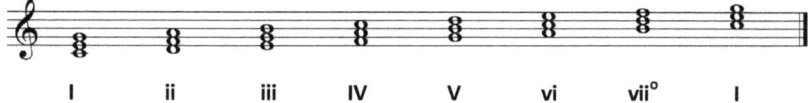

The I, IV, and V chords are represented by capital Roman numerals because they are major triads. The ii, iii, and vi chords are designated by lower case Roman numerals because they are minor triads. The vii° chord is characterized by a lower case Roman numeral with a degree sign because it is a diminished triad, which consists of two minor 3rds and a diminished 5th. An augmented triad consists of two major 3rds and an augmented 5th. This type of triad does not occur naturally in major or minor keys.

Triadic Harmony

The following example illustrates the triads of the key of *a* minor. Play these on your keyboard.

Example 33

i   ii°   III   iv   v   VI   VII   i

In all but two instances, the triads that were major in the major key are minor here, and vice versa; the ii° chord here is diminished, and the VII chord is major.

K.   MUSIC ANALYSIS

This Western system of triadic harmony is prevalent in the music from the Russian and other Slavic traditions. The Byzantine tradition, which utilizes a more linear system of singing in modes, will be discussed later. Play the following example on your keyboard. If possible, gather some singers from your choir, play the initial triad pitches for them, and sing the example.

Example 34

This arrangement of the First Antiphon is a standard one used in choirs utilizing the Russian system of tones. The key signature of one flat indicates that this arrangement is either in the key of *F* major or the key of *d* minor. Since the final chord of this line is an *F* major triad, it is most likely in the key of *F* major.

The basses are on an *F* on "Bless the", tenors are on an *A*, altos are on a *C*, and sopranos are on an *F*. This triad, *F*, *A*, *C*, is the I chord in the key of *F* major. This can be indicated by writing a "I" underneath the bass staff at the word "Bless". On "Lord", there is a 7th chord on the fifth degree of the scale (***C***, ***E***, ***G***, ***B**^b*). This, then, is a V^7 ("five-seven") chord. On the second half note of the word "Lord", the music returns to a I chord, and stays there until the word "soul". The second quarter note of the word "O" has a ***G*** in the soprano and a ***B**^b* in the tenor. Since they do not comprise part of the ***F*** major triad but are tones that pass between the chord tones, are known as ***passing tones***.[27]

On the word "soul", there is a ***B**^b* in both the bass and soprano parts, a ***D*** in the tenor part, and an ***F*** in the alto part. This is a ***B**^b* triad (***B**^b*, ***D***, ***F***), which is a IV chord in the key of ***F*** major. With the words "You are", the music returns to a I chord: ***F***, ***A***, ***C***. On "blest, O", there is another V^7 chord (***C***, ***E***, ***G***, ***B**^b*). On the final word, "Lord", the music ends on a I chord (***F***, ***A***, ***C***) in the key of ***F*** major. The following example illustrates this again, with the chord designations written beneath the grand staff.

---

[27]*Theory*, pp. 171-172. Cf., *Materials*, p. 106.

Example 35

The system of writing chord designations beneath the staff is known as ***figured bass***.[28]

The following example is of a hymn in a minor key.

---

[28] *Materials*, p. 226f.

Triadic Harmony

Example 36

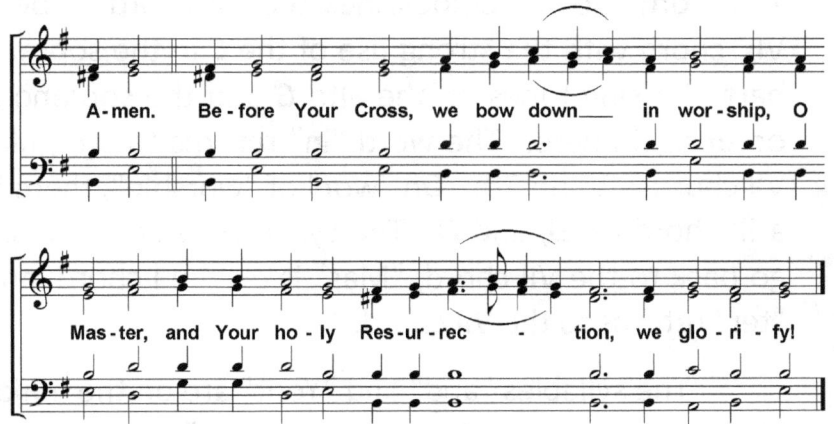

The key signature and the final chord reveal this to be in the key of *e* minor. The first chord on the "Amen", *B*, *D#*, and *F#*, is a major V chord. As seen in Example 56 above, the v chord occurs naturally as a minor chord in a minor key. Often, though, the 3rd of the v chord, which is the seventh degree of the minor scale (in this case, *D*) is raised one half step (here, *D* to *D#*). This is so it will act, not as a subtonic, but as a leading tone to the tonic of the minor key (in this example, *E*).

The second syllable of "Amen" is a i chord on *E*, *G*, and *B*. The phrase "Before Your Cross" alternates the V and the i chords twice. On "we", a VII occurs on

D, ***F#***, and ***A***. This is also in effect on "bow", with alto and soprano passing tones on ***G*** and ***B***, respectively. The word "down" embellishes the VII chord to be a VII^7 chord with the strong use of the ***C*** in the soprano part. Passing tones on the alto ***G*** and the soprano ***B*** occur again here. The word "in" returns to a regular VII chord with no 7th. On "wor" of "worship", there is a III chord, ***G***, ***B***, and ***D***. The syllables "ship" and "O" go back to the VII chord, "Mas" is on the i chord, and "ter" returns to the VII chord.

The syllables "and" and "Your" are on the major III chord, "ho" is on the VII chord, and "ly" is on the i chord. With the exception of passing tones, the word "Resurrection" is on the major V chord, (even though the raised 3rd, ***D#***, is missing on "rec"), with the prominent 7th, ***A***, on "rec". The syllable "glo" of "glorify" has ***A***, ***C***, ***E***, and ***G***, a 7th chord built on the fourth degree of the scale, or a iv^7 chord. The syllable "ri" is on a V chord, and the phrase ends with "fy" on the minor i chord.

The following is the example with its figured bass.

Example 37

Music analysis of this type will not be required of often by Orthodox choir directors and singers. However, becoming familiar with this analysis will assist in deciphering chords in order to give pitches to the choir.

The following exercises reinforce the concepts of keys, scales, triads, and chords that were discussed here.

EXERCISES • CHAPTER 3

1. Using the pattern of whole steps and half steps for major scales as a guide, construct the following scales. Use the ascending half of the scale only. Any questions as to the use of sharps or flats will be clarified in parentheses.

    A) *G* major (sharps)   B) *B^b* major
    C) *E^b* major   D) *D* major (sharps)
    E) *A* major (sharps)   F) *F* major (flats)
    G) *E* major (sharps)   H) *F$^\#$* major
    I) *D^b* major   J) *A^b* major
    K) *C$^\#$* major   L) *C^b* major
    M) *C* major   N) *B* major (sharps)
    O) *G^b* major

2. Using the pattern of whole steps and half steps for minor scales as a guide, construct the following scales. Again, use the ascending half of the scale only.

    A) *d* minor (flats)   B) *b* minor (sharps)
    C) *c* minor (flats)   D) *g* minor (flats)
    E) *e* minor (sharps)   F) *f* minor (flats)

Triadic Harmony

G) $g^\#$ minor (sharps)
H) a minor
I) $f^\#$ minor
J) $a^\#$ minor
K) $c^\#$ minor
L) b^b minor
M) e^b minor
N) $d^\#$ minor
O) a^b minor

3. Write out the pattern of whole steps and half steps for a major scale.

4. Write out the pattern of whole steps and half steps for a minor scale.

5. Write out the key signatures for the following minor scales.

A) c minor
B) b minor
C) d minor
D) e minor
E) g minor
F) a minor
G) $g^\#$ minor
H) f minor
I) $a^\#$ minor
J) $f^\#$ minor
K) e^b minor
L) b^b minor
M) $c^\#$ minor
N) a^b minor
O) $d^\#$ minor

6. Write out the key signatures for these scales.

   A) **A** major
   B) **F** major
   C) **E^b** major
   D) **G** major
   E) **B^b** major
   F) **D** major
   G) **C$^\sharp$** major
   H) **A^b** major
   I) **D^b** major
   J) **F$^\sharp$** major
   K) **E** major
   L) **G^b** major
   M) **B** major
   N) **C** major
   O) **C^b** major

7. For the following major scales, give the letter name of the note that corresponds to the solfege syllable it that particular key.

   A) **E^b** major: **Do**
   B) **G** major: **Sol**
   C) **F** major: **Mi**
   D) **A** major: **Ti**
   E) **B^b** major: **La**
   F) **A^b** major: **Fa**
   G) **D** major: **Re**
   H) **G^b** major: **La**
   I) **B** major: **Do**
   J) **E** major: **Ti**
   K) **C^b** major: **Mi**
   L) **F$^\sharp$** major: **Sol**
   M) **C$^\sharp$** major: **Fa**
   N) **D^b** major: **La**
   O) **C** major: **Sol**
   P) **E^b** major: **Re**
   Q) **A** major: **Mi**
   R) **E** major: **Fa**
   S) **B^b** major: **La**
   T) **C** major: **Mi**

Triadic Harmony

8. For the following minor scales, give the letter name of the note that corresponds to the solfege syllable in that particular key.

A) *a* minor: **Re**
B) *g* minor: **Ti**
C) *e* minor: **La**
D) *c* minor: **Do**
E) *b* minor: **Fa**
F) *g* minor: **Mi**
G) *b^b* minor: **Sol**
H) *a^b* minor: **Fa**
I) *f$^\#$* minor: **Re**
J) *g$^\#$* minor: **La**
K) *c$^\#$* minor: **Do**
L) *d* minor: **Mi**
M) *f* minor: **Fa**
N) *a* minor: **La**
O) *d$^\#$* minor: **Sol**
P) *e* minor: **Ti**
Q) *b^b* minor: **Re**
R) *a$^\#$* minor: **Fa**
S) *c* minor: **Mi**
T) *a^b* minor: **Sol**

9. Given the following keys, construct the chord called for on the treble staff, in root position.

A) *F* major: I chord
B) *e* minor: III chord
C) *C* major: V chord
D) *a* minor: iv chord
E) *d* minor: VI chord
F) *G* major: vii° chord
G) *e^b* minor: ii° chord
H) *F$^\#$* major: V chord
I) *G^b* major: vi chord
J) *a^b* minor: VII chord
K) *B^b* major: iii chord
L) *c$^\#$* minor: v chord
M) *b* minor: i chord
N) *A* major: vii° chord

O) *a#* minor: iv chord
Q) *B* major: V chord
S) *C♭* major: III chord

P) *E♭* major: ii chord
R) *f* minor: III chord
T) *c* minor: VI chord

10. List all of the intervals used in the following types of triads, from the bottom up.

A) major
D) augmented
B) minor
E) minor 7th chord
C) diminished

11. Explain how to determine if a triad is major.

12. Explain how to determine if a triad is minor.

13. Write out the following triads in first inversion in an SATB (soprano, alto, tenor, bass) setting.

A) *C* major B) *d* minor C) *B♭* major D) *e* minor
E) *D* major F) *g* minor G) *F#* major H) *a♭* minor
I) *E♭* major J) *a#* minor K) *C#* major L) *f* minor
M) *A* major N) *g#* minor O) *E* major P) *b♭* minor
Q) *C♭* major R) *e♭* minor S) *B* major T) *a* minor

14. Write out the following triads in second inversion in an SATB setting.

A) *a* minor B) *F* major C) *g* minor D) *G* major
E) *b* minor F) *C#* major G) *e* minor H) *A♭* major
I) *d* minor J) *B* major K) *a♭* minor L) *D* major
M) *c#* minor N) *B♭* major O) *f* minor P) *G♭* major
Q) *c* minor R) *E* major S) *e♭* minor T) *C♭* major

15. Write out the following 7th chords in third inversion in an SATB setting. Use a minor 7th in the chords from the root.

A) *A* major B) *c* minor C) *E♭* major D) *f#* minor
E) *E* major F) *b* minor G) *A♭* major H) *a#* minor
I) *G* major J) *g#* minor K) *C#* major L) *f* minor
M) *F#* major N) *d#* minor O) *D* major P) *b♭* minor
Q) *F* major R) *e* minor S) *D♭* major T) *a♭* minor

16. Explain how to get to a relative minor key from a major key.

17. Write out the Roman numerals for the naturally occurring chords of a major key.

18.   Write out the Roman numerals for the naturally occurring chords of a minor key.

4
GIVING PITCHES

The ability to efficiently and accurately give pitches to a choir is one of the most important skills that a choir director will need to master. The correct singing of the liturgical hymns; the liturgical flow of the services; the confidence of the choir director in himself or herself; the confidence of the choir in the choir director; all of these factors are directly dependent on the important ability of the choir director to give pitches.

Before giving the pitches, the choir director must be aware of where each section of the choir is positioned. There are different "floor plans" that are used by various choirs to position their sections. The following example illustrates one of the most commonly used positionings for an SATB (soprano, alto, tenor, bass) choir.

Example 38

          Altos   **Sopranos**

Basses   **Tenors**

                Choir Director

This placement of the sections follows the pattern of a piano keyboard, with higher-pitched voices on the right and lower-pitched voices on the left. It is important to note that the choir director should face the singers when directing, and not the priest or the sanctuary. During longer prayers, such as the Anaphora, the choir director may then face the sanctuary and focus on the prayer being read.

Another item of importance for giving pitches is the tuning fork. The tuning fork is a necessary tool, especially for beginning choir directors, precisely because it provides a point of *reference* for the chord to be given. The stress here is on the reference, because singing a hymn in the key in which it is written is not a hard-and-fast rule. Other factors may enter into which key the hymn will be pitched in: the note that the priest, deacon or bishop is on; how many singers (and in which sections) are present for the given service; the weather (damp, rainy weather puts an added strain on the vocal cords); and the physical condition of the singers themselves (some may have colds or sore throats). Many experienced choir directors, after years of using the tuning fork and having a good tonal memory for the reference pitch, are able to effectively abandon the use of the tuning fork and give the pitches from memory. The standard tuning fork used by most Orthodox choir directors in parishes utilizing music in the Western triadic system is the one pitched on **C** at 523.3 vibrations per second. The tuning fork pitched on **A** at 440 vibrations per second can be used as a supplementary tool.

A. TRIADS

The Movable **Do** System of solfege singing as outlined in the previous chapter can be quite useful in giving pitches to a choir.

Example 39

This example illustrates a chord frequently found at the beginning of Orthodox hymns using the Western triadic system of harmony. The key signature of **B**^{b} tells us that this hymn is either in the key of *F* major or in the key of **d** minor. The basses have an **F**, the tenors are on a **C**, the altos also chord, we have **F**, **A**, **C**, or an **F** major triad. There is a good chance, then, that this hymn is in the key of **F** major.

It is customary to give the triad in descending order; that is, first give the **C** to the tenors, then give the **A** to the sopranos, and then give the **F** to both the altos and the basses. The reason for this is that, by ending on the root of the chord, a feel for the triad is reinforced. Using the Movable **Do** solfege syllables,

Giving Pitches

the choir director could sing the *C* on the syllable "*Sol*", the *A* on "*Mi*", and the *F* on "*Do*".

Example 40

The key signature of one sharp in this example indicates a key of either *G* major or *e* minor. The basses have a *G*, the tenors are on *D*, the altos come in on *G*, and the sopranos are singing a *B*. The notes of this chord, *G*, *B*, *D*, form a *G* major triad. The solfege syllables used to give this chord in descending order would be *Sol*, *Mi*, *Do*. Play Example 62, with its *F* major triad, without singing it; then, again without singing, play the *G* major triad as given in Example 63. Do this a few times, first by playing the notes successively as you would give them to the sections of the choir (tenors, sopranos, altos and basses), and then by playing the notes of each chord simultaneously. Notice the similarity in sound quality between the two triads. This is what makes the Movable *Do* System so valuable, because it associates the sound quality and patterns with the syllables. Once you become familiar with how a major triad sounds on the syllables *Sol*, *Mi*, *Do*, you will be able to select any note, and from that note sing a major triad by just using the syllables *Sol*, *Mi*, *Do*.

The Movable *Do* syllables can be useful in moving to a different key from the reference tone of the tuning fork. For example, to give the *G* major triad in Example 63 from a *C* tuning fork, you could play the note *C* on the tuning fork and call it *Do*; then, by singing "*Do*, *Re*" in your mind, you would reach the note *D* on the syllable *Re*. Renaming the note *D* as the syllable *Sol*, you would then sing the pitches of a *G* major triad (*D*, *B*, *G*) on the syllables *Sol*, *Mi*, *Do*.

Giving Pitches

Example 41

Another common voicing for the major triad is given below.

Example 42

Here, the 5th of the triad, **C**, is in the alto and the 3rd, **A**, is in the tenor, with the root, **F**, in both the soprano and the bass. One way to give this pitch is to sing down the chord in your mind to the root on **F**. Give this note to the sopranos, then go up to the tenors for the **A**. Since the sopranos do not normally have their note in the beginning chord, come back to them and give them their **F** again for reinforcement. Go down to the **C** for the altos, and back up to the **F** for the basses. The following, with the notes in parentheses being the ones you "sing" in your mind, would be the order of pitches given: (**C**, **A**,) **F**, **A**, **F**, **C**, **F**. Another way to give this set of pitches is to start with the **F** for the sopranos, go up to the **A** for the tenors, **back to the F** for the sopranos, down to the **C** for the altos, and then up to **F** for the basses. The order of pitches in this pattern, then, is: **F**, **A**, (**F**), **C**, **F**.

The following example illustrates some major triads in voicings as you would commonly find them in our Orthodox hymnography.

Giving Pitches

Example 43

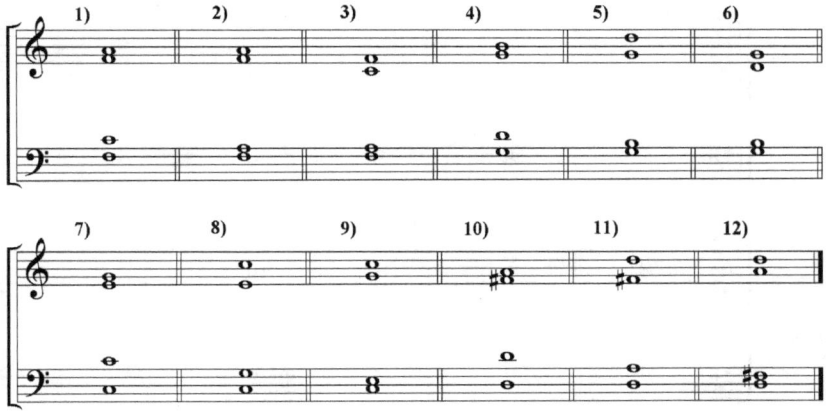

Items 1 through 3 are in the key of **F** major, items 4 through 6 are in the key of **G** major, items 7 through 9 are in the key of **C** major, and items 10 through 12 are in the key of **D** major. Practice singing these examples using the Movable *Do* solfege syllables, then check yourself by playing them on your keyboard. Remember to sing the parts in the following order: tenor, soprano, alto, and bass.

The following example illustrates some minor triads in voicings as you would commonly find them in our Orthodox hymnography.

Example 44

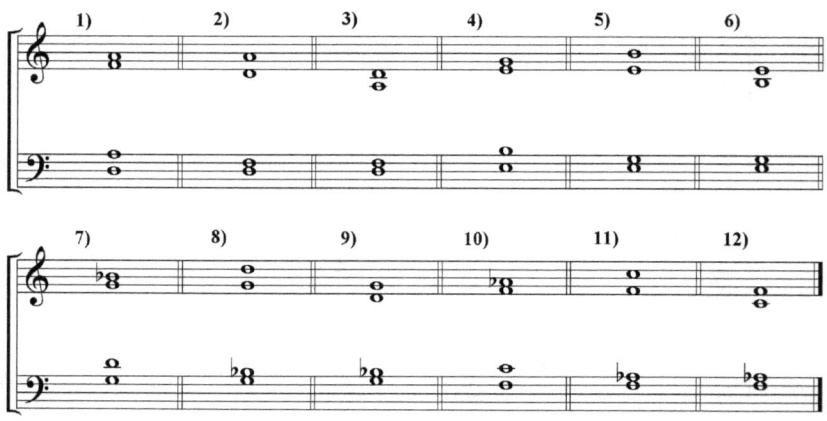

Items 1 through 3 are in the key of ***d*** minor; items 4 through 6 are in the key of ***e*** minor; items 7 through 9 are in the key of ***g*** minor; and items 10 through 12 are in the key of ***f*** minor. Again, practice giving these pitches off of a ***C*** tuning fork, then double-check them on your keyboard.

Giving Pitches

B. INVERSIONS

Chords in first, second, or third inversion are not as common in Orthodox hymnography as those found in root position. However, since they do sometimes occur, it is useful for the choir director to be able to easily recognize these chords and effectively give the pitches to the singers.

Example 45

The key signature of one sharp indicates either ***G*** major or ***e*** minor. The bass has a ***G***, the tenor has an ***E***, the alto also has an ***E***, and the soprano has a ***B***. Rearranging these chord tones into root position, there is ***E***, ***G***, ***B***, an ***e*** minor triad, with the 3rd, ***G***, in the bass. Since this is the key of ***e*** minor, the solfege syllables in descending order will ***not*** be ***Sol***, ***Mi***, ***Do***, but will be **Mi, Do, La**. Giving the pitches from tenor to soprano to alto to bass (with the parenthetical syllables representing those pitches to be sung in your mind), it would be **La, Mi, (Do,) La, Mi**. It would be advisable to end by repeating the root of the chord, **E**, on the syllable **La** for the altos, to reinforce the minor **e** triad.

C. 7TH CHORDS

Giving pitches for 7th chords will most likely occur for the previously discussed V^7 chord. Again, this chord consists of a major triad with a minor 7th added on.

Example 46

Here, the key is **F** major. The V^7 chord is made up of the notes **C**, **E**, **G**, and **B**^{b}. Many times, the 3rd on **E** is omitted in order to double up on the root of the chord, **C**. Since **C** is the 5th degree of the **F** major scale, it will have the solfege syllable **Sol**. Giving the pitches in descending order for this chord would encompass the following: **Sol**, **Fa**, **Re**, **Sol**. In the hymnography of the Russian tradition, this is the initial chord for stikhera tones 1 and 5, and for the tradition lenten litany melody.

EXERCISES • CHAPTER 4

The best ongoing exercise for giving pitches is to practice with as many hymns as possible, first identifying the key and corresponding initial chord (V chord in the key of **F** major, i chord in the key of *e* minor, etc.), working out the chord tones with the Movable **Do** solfege syllables, getting to the chord from the **C** on the tuning fork, singing the chord, and then comparing this with the chord as you play it on your keyboard. The more you practice, the sooner you will become proficient at giving pitches.

Utilize the following examples to practice giving pitches. After you try each one, check out how accurate you were by playing the selection on a keyboard.

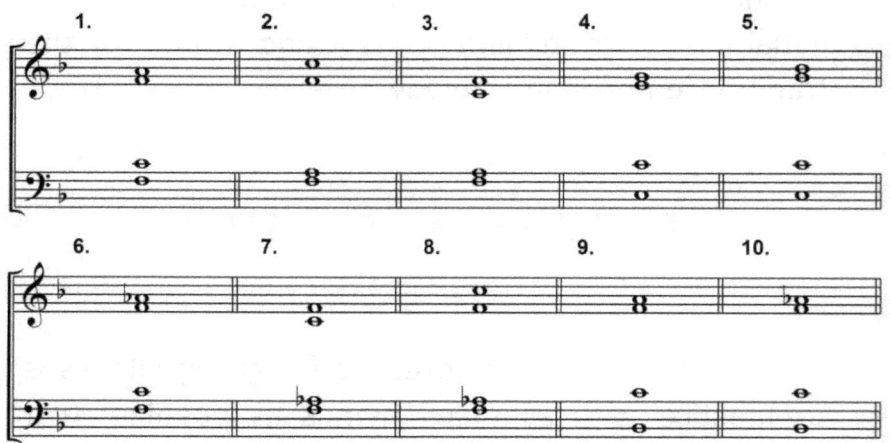

5
MELODY AND HARMONY

Melody is the horizontal set of pitches organized in time that determines the shape of a musical line.[1] As such, melody incorporates elements of both pitch and rhythm.

A. MOTIVES AND PHRASES

A *motive* is the smallest distinctive melodic germ, made up of a few tones and rhythms.[2] A *phrase* is a complete musical idea that ends with a cadence.[3] A *cadence* is a musical ending or closing section.[4] A motive, therefore, provides the melodic kernel of a phrase.

---

[1] *Theory*, p. 101.
[2] Ibid, p. 102.
[3] Ibid.
[4] *Materials*, p. 53f. Cf., *Theory*, p. 86f.

Example 47

The motive in this example, taken from an arrangement of the Cherubic Hymn by Gregory Lvovsky, is distinctive both in pitch and in rhythm. The rhythmic element consists of a dotted quarter note, followed by an eighth note, and then two quarter notes. A **dot** increases the value of a note or rest by one half.[5] Pitchwise, there is a **G**, followed by an **A**, then back to **G**, and descending to **F♯**. The shape of the motive forms an arch or curve, ascending and descending. The shape of a motive or phrase is called its **contour**.[6] This contour, combined with the specific rhythmic pattern, gives this motive its unique character and makes it recognizable, even when it occurs later in the hymn at a different pitch level.

---

[5] *Theory*, p. 13.
[6] *Materials*, p. 71f.

Melody and Harmony

Example 48

Here, the motive begins on an **A** rather than a **G**. However, it still retains its basic rhythmic pattern and melodic contour.

B. ANTECEDENT – CONSEQUENT PHRASES

There are patterns of phrases, which occur commonly in Orthodox liturgical music, which share a question-and-answer relationship with each other. Such phrases are called **antecedent-consequent phrases**.[7] They form an "A-B" type pattern, whereby the first, antecedent phrase is countered by the consequent phrase.

---

[7]*Materials*, p. 75. Cf., *Theory*, p. 104.

Example 49

This example is a tone 3 setting for "Lord, I Call Upon You" from the Common Chant tones of the Russian tradition. The first phrase can stand by itself. Musically, however, there is a feeling of incompleteness, a feeling that the music needs to be resolved to a complete ending. This is accomplished in the second phrase, where the cadence on "Lord" gives the feeling of resolution and "answers" the first phrase.

C. MONOPHONY

Harmony is the chordal or vertical structure of a musical composition.[8] Whereas melody is constructed horizontally with the elements of pitch and rhythm, harmony uses intervals, triads, and

---

[8]*Harvard*, p. 371, under "Harmony".

chords as its basic tools. There are a variety of harmonic textures that is found in Orthodox liturgical music.

Monophony is music consisting of a single melodic line without additional parts or accompaniment.[9]

Example 50

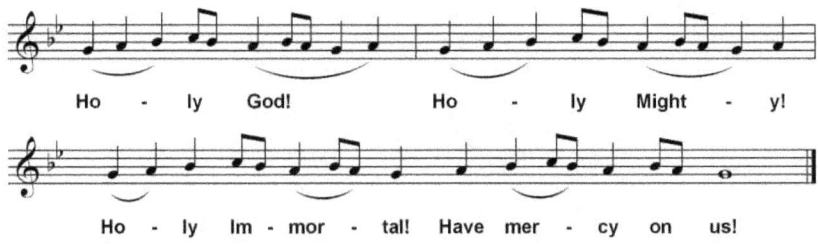

There is a lack of vertical harmony or intervals in this example. The simple, horizontal melody makes it easy to teach to children, and also aids in prayerful concentration on the words of the hymn.

---

[9]Ibid, p. 539, under "Monophony, monophonic".

D. DIOPHONY

Diophony is music consisting of a single melodic line with a second line that is not melodic.[10] Diophonic music often makes use of an **ison**, a repeated tone which functions as a reference pitch for the melody.[11]

Example 51

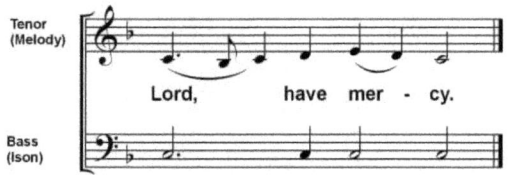

---

[10] Many music theory textbooks loosely categorize this harmonic texture as "monophonic". However, it is *not* strict monophony. Because of its historic prevalence in Byzantine chant, this harmonic texture can be aptly called "diophonic", a term first coined by Dr. Vladimir Morosan.

[11] Wellecz, Egon, *Byzantine Music and Hymnography*, 2nd Edition, Oxford at the Clarendon Press, Oxford, England, 1980 (hereafter referred to as "*Byzantine*"), p. 16.

The symbol below the treble clef, *8* (which could also be rendered *8va-*), indicates that the tenor part is sung an octave lower than written. This eliminates the need for ledger lines. The tenor has the melody, as indicated. The ison in the bass part, on the note *C*, does not function as accompaniment in the Western sense of harmonic chords, but serves as a point of reference for the melody, which is focused on the note *C*. This example of Byzantine chant, then, is not in the "key" of *C* (major or minor). However, since the focus of the melody and the ison does center around this note, this example is in the **modality** of *C*, making using of the Byzantine system of modes.

E. HOMOPHONY

Homophony is music consisting of a single melodic line with harmonic accompaniment.[12] Most Orthodox liturgical music that uses the Western triadic system of harmony is homophonic.

---

[12]*Harvard*, p. 390, under "Homophony". Cf., *Materials*, p. 116f.

Example 52

The melody in this example is in the soprano. The tenor has a harmonization of the melody, up a 3rd. The contour of this harmonization parallels that of the melody. The alto and bass parts are filling in chord tones. Homophonic music is the easiest texture to analyze chord progressions using figured bass.

F. POLYPHONY

Polyphony is a musical texture consisting of two or more independent melodies or lines.[13] It can be the use of two different melodies, or the use of the

---

[13]*Harvard*, p. 687, under "Polyphony". Cf., *Materials*, p. 116f.

Melody and Harmony

same melody sung by different voices at different times.

Example 53

Here, the sopranos and altos share the same basic melody, but at different times and at different pitch levels. The soprano part is centered around the note ***B***, while the alto part is centered around the note ***G***. Because of its more complex structure, which can tend to distract from liturgical prayer and worship, the polyphonic texture is used with restraint in Orthodox liturgical music.

EXERCISES • CHAPTER 5

The best exercises you can do in relation to the concepts discussed in this chapter are to apply them throughout your years as a choir director. Each time you are going to direct or rehearse a hymn, become familiar with the melodic elements of pitch and rhythm found within the motives, the melodic kernels that make up the melody. See where the musical phrases occur, and if there is any relationship between them, such as found with antecedent-consequent phrases. Identify the type of harmonic texture the hymn is composed in, whether it be monophonic, diophonic, homophonic, or polyphonic. As you gradually integrate these various elements into your experience, you will bring the musical expression of the hymn forward and manifest the beauty of our Orthodox liturgical hymnography.

6
CONDUCTING THE CHOIR

The abilities to effectively conduct a choir during the liturgical services and efficiently run a choir rehearsal are basic skills that a choir director needs to master. Conducting a choir involves familiarity with the conducting plane and the beat patterns used in the conducting of the hymnography.

Before covering that material, however, it is important to address one issue that confronts all directors. Some directors prefer to sing with their choirs while conducting. Others feel it is best not to, since, by keeping silent, the director can listen to and adjust the singers concerning balance and blend. One thought should be kept in mind, though. If you do choose to keep silent as a director, then you should **at least** mouth the words of the text of the hymnology along with your choir members who are singing it. Otherwise, you will seem elitist, appearing to your choir members as someone who is "too good" to be bothered singing with them.

The **conducting plane** is the area in space in which the conductor moves his or her hands.[1] The vertical portion of the plane extends from the crown of the head to about waist level. The horizontal part covers the area between the perimeters of the arms as they hang naturally by the side of the body. This is shown in the example on the following page.

Example 54

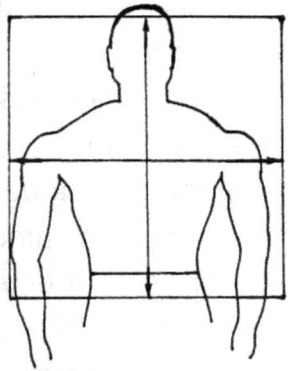

---

[1]Rudolf, Max, *The Grammar of Conducting*, 2nd Edition, Schirmer Books, Macmillan Publishing Company, Inc, New York, NY, 1980 (hereafter referred to as "*Grammar*"), pp. xviii and 1.

A. BEAT PATTERNS

There are three basic beat patterns that are used most frequently in the conducting of our hymnography.[2] One of these, the 4-pattern, utilizes all four directions of the conducting plane: **down**, **left**, **right**, **up**.

Example 54

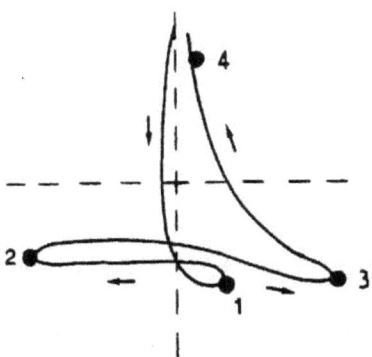

Notice that the graph illustrates a conducting style that involves a smooth change of direction from one beat to another. Although some music may, at times, call for an abrupt, snappy moving of the hands,

---

[2]Ibid, pp. 1-10, 35-43, and 61-67.

this style in general is more appropriate for instrumental music. The vocal character of our Orthodox hymnography calls for a smoother style of hand movement.

Hand position is very important in determining a comfortable, relaxed style of conducting. Generally, the hand should be held in front of the body, palm down, with the fingers kept close together but not pressing into each other. All movement should be at the wrist, not in the elbow or upper arm.

Example 55

 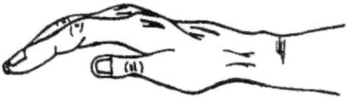

The important thing to remember in developing a comfortable hand position is to hold it naturally and relax. Tension and unnatural positioning of the hands leads to many conducting problems.

Another basic beat pattern is the 2-pattern. It resembles a backwards letter "J". The downward movement ends at the right side of the waist, and the upward movement culminates at the crown of the head. The directions for the 2-pattern, then, are: **down, up**.

Example 56

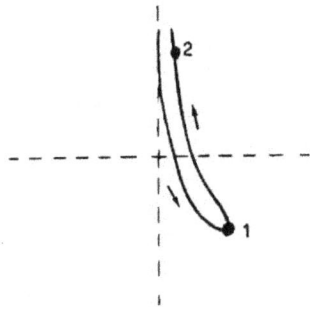

The 3-pattern begins moving in the opposite direction than the 4-pattern did. After the downbeat, the 4-pattern moved to the left. The 3-pattern moves to the right after the downbeat, and then finishes with an upward movement to the crown of the head. The directions for a 3-pattern are: **down, right, up.**

Example 57

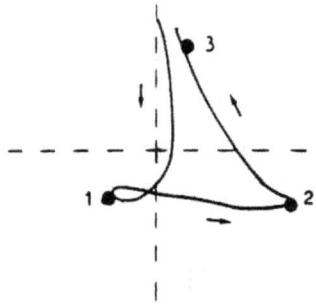

These three basic beat patterns should be comfortably mastered before applying them to any conducting style.

B. CHANT STYLE

The strict, metered style of conducting, in which each measure contains the same number of beats, is found and used the least in our Orthodox hymnography. The two conducting styles utilized the most for our liturgical music are the chant style and the stikhera style.

The **chant style** of conducting uses combinations of different meters that are organized according to the *text*.[3] In other words, it is the way the **accents of the text** occur that determines where musical downbeats will occur and, therefore, what combination of meter patterns will be used.

Primary textual accents, then, must occur on the downbeats. In singing the initial "Amen" of any service, for example, the downbeat must be on the syllable "men", since this is where the accent of the word is found. Using the four possible directions of conducting (down, left, right, and up), the first syllable of the "Amen" should be directed with a beat going up. Before singing that first syllable, however, the

---

[3]Lamb, Gordon H., *Choral Techniques*, William C. Brown Company, Dubuque, IA, 1976, p. 141.

choir must be prepared to sing by directing a beat which will both show them the speed at which they will be singing and give them an opportunity to take a breath beforehand. This beat is called the ***preparation beat***.⁴ Using arrows to determine the direction of the conductor's hands, the following example illustrates how the "Amen" is to be conducted.

Example 58

| A - men.

The arrow within the parentheses symbolizes the preparation beat, on which nothing is sung. By moving on the preparation beat to the right, the hand is then in the natural position to move up on the first syllable of "Amen", and then come down for a downbeat on the second, accented syllable.

---

⁴*Grammar*, pp. 4-5.

If the first syllable to be sung was accented, as in the word "Glory", the preparation beat would be going up, so as to have a downbeat on the accented syllable.

Example 59

$$(\rightarrow) \quad \downarrow$$

Glo - ry

To direct the entrance of a hymn, then, it is important to find where the initial downbeat will occur (on the first accented syllable), and then **back up** in the sequence of beat patterns (down, up, right, left) until coming to the preparation beat.

The following example illustrates a hymn that can be examined in applying the chant style of conducting.

Example 60

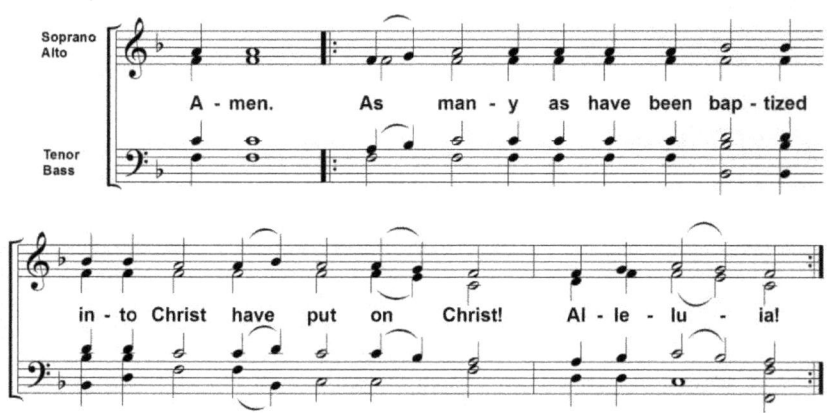

Saying the text out loud, primary accents can be found on the following syllables: the second syllable of "Amen"; the first syllable of "many"; the first syllable of "baptized"; "Christ"; "put"; the second word "Christ"; the third syllable of "Alleluia". To direct this with a beat on each quarter note would make it plodding and heavy. Using the half note as the basic beat would render the singing of this hymn much smoother. Many hymns in the chant style use the half note as the basic beat.

The quarter note at the beginning of the word "Amen" comes in on the second half of a half note beat. To give a preparation beat on only the first half of a beat, the drop preparation beat is used. This consists in holding your hand straight out in front of you, at mid chest level, and dropping the wrist and forearm to waist level. When the hand starts moving ***up*** from the waist back to the crown of the head, this is where the second half of the beat occurs and where the singing begins. On the second syllable of "Amen", a 1-beat should be used. This is done by dropping the hand from forehead to waist and back to forehead again, almost in a circular motion if seen from the side of the body. Since the next downbeat occurs on the first syllable of "many", the hand must move up on the word "as". Therefore, the cut-off for the 1-beat at the end of "Amen" should move to the right.

Example 61

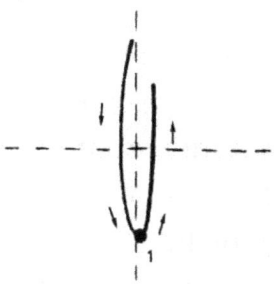

From the downbeat on "many" to the downbeat on "baptized", there are three half-note values. Thus, a 3-pattern will be used on "many". From the downbeat on "baptized" to the downbeat on "Christ", there are two-and-a-half half-note values. On "baptized", then, an *extended* 2-pattern will be used. Since a secondary accent is found on the first syllable of "into", this will be the point where the second half of the 2-pattern (where the hand will move up) will begin. The extension, then, is on the first half of the pattern. To get the feel of the extension, count "1, 2" on each half of the 2-pattern; that is, "1, 2" as your hand moves down and "1, 2" as your hand moves up. Then, without changing the speed of your counting, count "1, 2, 3" on the downbeat. To do this, you will have to *extend* your hand further down on the downbeat, at the point of the curve of the backwards "J". Practice doing this while singing, "baptized", giving the first syllable a half-note value and the second syllable a quarter-note value. Start bringing your hand up (for the second half of the beat" on the two syllables for "into".

From "Christ" to "put", there are two half-note values, as there are between "put" and the second word "Christ", and again between "Christ" and the third syllable of "Alleluia". All of these downbeats, then, will have 2-patterns. Since this hymn is repeated, and the music calls for an upbeat on "as" back at the beginning, a 4-pattern should be used on the third syllable of "Alleluia", except for the last time, when a 3-pattern will be used to end the hymn. This will result in the last syllable of "Alleluia", which is an unaccented syllable, being directed to the right, enabling a smooth cut-off.

The following example illustrates the hymn again, with markings for the downbeats and beat patterns to be used. The arrow with a dot above it in parentheses at the beginning stands for the drop preparation beat. The marking of "x2" over the word "baptized" indicates an extended 2-pattern. The little notch over the word "into" shows where the second half of the 2-pattern (where your hand comes back up) begins. On "Alleluia", the 4-pattern is to be used, except for the final time, where the 3-pattern is indicated.

Example 62

This one example contains all the elements needed to direct the chant style of conducting. It is important to reiterate that where the primary textual accents occur is where the downbeats will be placed. Then, calculating how many beats are between each downbeat will determine what type of beat pattern will be assigned at each downbeat. Determining the preparation beat is vital to a smooth entrance. The use of a drop preparation, a 1-beat, and an extended beat may be called for, at times. Finally, a smooth cut-off guards against an abrupt ending to the singing. There are many different styles of cut-offs. The following example illustrates one that is both smooth and does not call attention to itself. It is done by keeping the hand palm down, and slightly bouncing the bottom of the palm. The cadence syllable is the last one sung.

Example 63

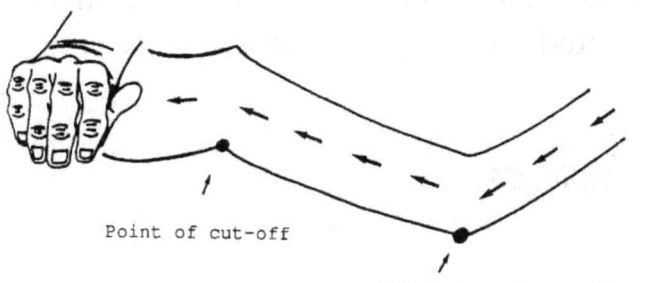

Point of cut-off

Point of cadence syllable

C. STIKHERA STYLE

The stikhera style of conducting is used when singing stikhera (verses) in which there are many syllables on one tone (recitative), followed by held tones at the cadence. The beginning of the verse would begin the same as a hymn in the chant style; that is, the first downbeat would be identified, and the four directions of the beat pattern would be backed up until reaching the preparation beat. For the recitative portion of the verse, a more subdued version of the 1-pattern would be called for. The conductor's hand would "bob" downward on the accented syllables, as a buoy bobs on water.

Example 64

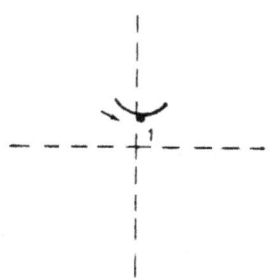

Before assigning beat patterns to the cadences, it is necessary to identify where the held tones would occur according to the *musical* pattern of the tone being sung and the *textual* accents occurring at the beginning and end of the verses.

Example 65

Accept our evening prayers, O holy Lord.

Grant us remission of our sins, //

For You alone have manifested Your Resurrection to the world.

The double virgule at the end of the second line (//) indicates that this line is the last phrase pattern before the cadence phrase.

Using the musical patterns for Russian stikhera tone 1, this text can be marked as follows.

Example 66

Ac<u>**cept**</u> **our evening prayers, O** <u>**ho**</u>**ly Lord.**

Grant us re<u>**mis**</u>**sion of our sins, //**

For You alone have manifested Your Resur<u>**rec**</u>**tion to the world.**

Analyzing this stikheron using the stikhera style, we find that the initial accent is on the second syllable of "accept". A drop preparation would be a good choice, since the first syllable would only use half a beat, using the half note as the basic beat, as is customary to do in the stikhera style. The secondary accent would be on the first syllable of "evening". An extended 1-beat on the second syllable of "accept" would be appropriate. Another secondary accent occurs on prayers. These can be marked by vertical notches (|). It would be at these points that the smaller 1-beat would "bob" down as you direct the choir. Another extended 1-beat could be assigned to the first syllable of "holy", ensuring a downbeat on "Lord".

On the second line, "grant" is a secondary, recitative accent, as is the word "of". Therefore, assigning an extended 2-beat to the second syllable of "remission" would bring the hand back up (for the second half of the beat) on the word "of". Since this line is not a complete sentence, but is completed by the third line, there should be no break in the singing or breathing at this point in the music. By assigning an extended 1-beat to "sins" at the end of the second line, the hand will come down for the secondary accent on "You" at the beginning of the third line. Other secondary accents in this line are the second syllable of "alone", the first and third syllables of "manifested", and the first syllable of "Resurrection". Using an extended 2-beat on the third syllable of "Resurrection" will bring about the desired downbeat on the word "world".

The following example illustrates how the choir director's sheet might be marked for directing this stikheron.

Example 67

     x1 | | x1   1

Ac<u>cept</u> our evening prayers, O <u>ho</u>ly Lord.

 | x2   x1

Grant us re<u>mis</u>sion of our sins, //

  | | | | | x2 | 1

For You alone have manifes<u>t</u>ed Your Resur<u>rec</u>tion to the world.

By using the subtle 1-beat for the secondary accents of the recitative and actual beat patterns for entrances and cadences, the music of the stikhera style is smoothly sung while properly accentuating the text.

EXERCISES • CHAPTER 6

Mastery of the beat patterns used in conducting should be the initial task of the director. After this, review, practice, and application of the chant and stikhera styles of conducting should be repeated. The more you practice, the easier this becomes, and the more confident you will become in directing your choir for having mastered these skills. Taking a vocal conducting course, or having a more experienced choir director guide you along, can also prove to be beneficial.

II. REHEARSING ORTHODOX LITURGICAL MUSIC

7
BEGINNING THE CHOIR REHEARSAL

Having examined and articulated the basics of singing, triadic harmony, and choral conducting, we now turn to the specifics of organizing and carrying out the choir rehearsal. A complete and thorough rehearsal should be comprised of three elements: the spiritual, the liturgical, and the musical. Only by incorporating all three aspects can Church singers be prepared and competent to execute the wonderful *ministry* of liturgical music to which they are called.

The first thing that must be said concerning the success of having choir rehearsals is they must be both *regular* and *consistent*. By "regular" we mean they must be scheduled on a regular basis on the same day and time. Some parish choirs find it convenient to rehearse on a weeknight, say, on Tuesday evenings beginning at 7 pm. Other parishes, especially those whose members live further away from the church, find it easier to hold rehearsals before the Resurrectional Vespers service, say, on Saturday afternoons beginning at 3 pm. An effective length for a rehearsal should be about two to two-and-a-half hours. Anything less would minimize the productivity of the rehearsal, and anything more would prove overbearing and exhausting on the part of the singers. By "consistent" we mean that rehearsals should be held on a consistently maintained schedule, such as every week or every other week (say, the first and third or second and fourth weeks of the month). Holding rehearsals in a haphazard manner (for example, two weeks in a row, then nothing for four or five weeks, then two weeks in a row again) causes confusion to the singers, who cannot rely on a definite schedule to fit the rehearsals into an already busy lifestyle. Trusting in a rehearsal schedule that is consistent will ensure that your singers can be counted on to be present at the maximum amount of rehearsals they can possibly attend.

A.   OPENING PRAYER

As previously stated, the **calling _from_ _God_** to engage in liturgical singing is a **_ministry_**. As such, it is more than appropriate for the choir director to begin each rehearsal with an opening prayer. There are many possibilities for such prayers to choose from (such as the Lord's Prayer). One prayer that has been found appropriate for the beginning of choir rehearsals is the following:

"O Christ our God, Who said, "Where two or three are gathered in My Name, there am I in the midst of them!", look down upon us now as we begin this choir rehearsal! Grant us to prayerfully master the music, with which we will worship You liturgically! May we perfect our singing in order to praise and glorify Your all – honorable and majestic Name: of the Father, and of the Son, and of the Holy Spirit, now and ever and unto ages of ages! Amen."

This prayer has a few key elements in it. First of all, it acknowledges the centrality of our Lord, Jesus Christ. Second, it quotes our Lord Himself directly from the Gospels. Third, it points seriously to the ministry of liturgical music and the need for prayerful preparation and mastery of the musical skills involved. Finally, it manifests the goal of all worship: the praise and glorification of the one God in the Holy Trinity: God the Father, the Son of God, and the Holy Spirit of God. A prayer such as this one, said by the choir director as he or she and all the singers bow their heads towards the holy sanctuary of the church, sets the correct spiritual tone and perspective for the serious work about to be done within the rehearsal.

B. WARM – UP EXERCISES

After the opening prayer, it is best to begin the actual singing portion of the rehearsal with some vocal warm-up exercises. As mentioned previously,[1] an appropriate start can be with exercises that teach and reinforce the basic concepts of posture, breathing, and tone placement. Other warm-up exercises may then follow.

One exercise that helps open up the throat and aids in good breath support is to sing the first five notes of a major scale up and then down, followed by a hold on the bottom note up a half-step. Then, using this raised half-step as the start of a new major scale, the singers would go up and

---

[1] Cf. above, the Exercises in chapter 2, pp. 20-23.

down the first five notes of the new scale, ending on a hold on the bottom note of the new scale up a half-step again. This, in turn, begins the five-note process on a new scale. This can ascend until the singers are at the top of their **comfortable** range, that is, able to maintain good breath support and an open throat. They can then reverse the process by singing up and down the five notes of the major scale, ending on a hold a half-step below the ending note. A new scale then begins a half-step down, etc., until the bottom of the **comfortable** range for the singers is reached. Singing the notes on a **<u>non-solfege</u>** syllable (such as "doo") will free up the singers' concentration so they may focus on their proper singing techniques. The beginning of this warm-up exercise is illustrated in the following example.

Example 68

etc.

This exercise should be sung legato (a smooth, connected style) so that any choppiness in the singing and shallowness of breathing may be avoided. Conducting this on a 1-beat for each whole note value can reinforce this and ensure a consistent rhythm for the exercise, as seen below.

Example 69

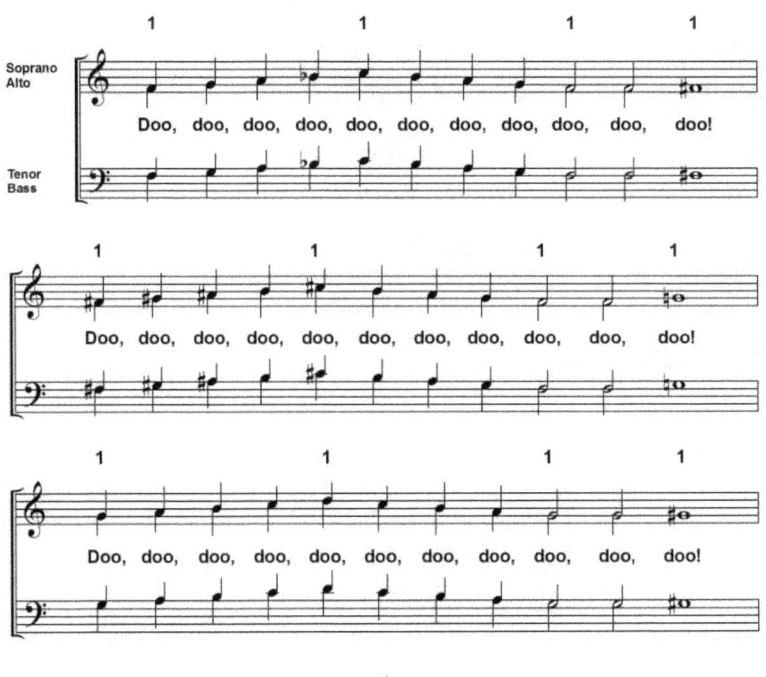

etc.

Again, this is an excellent warm-up exercise that can be comfortably done completely in the first five minutes of the rehearsal.

A parallel warm-up exercise is the reverse of this. Have the singers begin on the fifth tone of a major scale, singing down to the first tone (tonic) and back up to the fifth, finishing by holding on a note a half-step **below** the fifth of the first scale. The next descending-and-ascending five-note scale will be in a key a half-step below the first one. Again, end by holding on a tone a half-step below the fifth of the second scale. Continue in this manner until you reach the bottom of the singers' **comfortable** range, then work your way back up again. This is illustrated as follows:

Example 70

Once again, have the choir members sing this legato, and conduct it on a 1-beat for each whole note value, as follows:

Example 71

etc.

Again, this warm-up exercise can be comfortably completed in five minutes of the rehearsal time.

A third warm-up exercise is to have the choir members sing on the syllable "doo" on an **F** major chord, with the tenors on the **C**, the sopranos on the **A**, and both the altos and the basses on the **F**. This is illustrated below.

Example 72

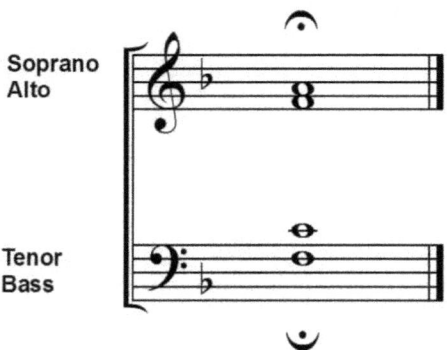

Notice the fermata (⌢) placed above and below the whole notes in this example. The reason for this is that the singers will be holding this note consistently for the next five minutes (instruct your singers to breathe when necessary during this time), while you, as the choir director, will be gesturing with your hands for each of the various sections to alternately sing louder and softer. The benefit of this exercise (besides that of strengthening the muscles of the diaphragm as they sustain the held tone) is it begins training your choir members to listen to each other, to be aware of the balance and blend of which section's note is louder and which is softer. Before beginning this exercise, you can explain this to your singers and ask them to see if, when their section is singing a louder note, they can hear which section or sections is/are singing a softer note. This also has the further advantage of getting your choir members used to watching you and your directions as you conduct the choir. You will find that practicing this exercise for a full five minutes of your rehearsal will both sensitize your singers to listen to the other sections of the choir more carefully for balance and blend, and also condition them to follow your direction more closely during the liturgical services.

Returning to warm-up exercises involving scale runs, the following combine these runs with the triad of a I chord (tonic chord) in each key. Again, using the syllable "doo", start on the 5th of the I chord, descend to the 3rd, then the root, then proceed step-wise up the major scale to the 5th again, holding on a tone a half-step ***below*** the 5th, to descend. Continue this in the singer's ***comfortable*** range, then work your way back up, as follows:

Example 73

etc.

Conduct this legato, on a 1 beat, using the half note as the basic beat, as follows:

Example 74

etc.

This can be turned into a separate exercise by beginning on the root of the chord and reversing direction, going up to the 3rd and then the 5th before coming down step-wise to the root again, holding on a tone a half-step *above* the root, as follows:

Example 75

etc.

Again, conduct this legato on a 1-beat, using the half note as the basic beat, as follows:

Example 76

etc.

Choosing from just three of these warm-up exercises alone for five minutes each will take up only fifteen minutes of your choir rehearsal. You can alternate any of these exercises with the ones enumerated in chapter 2 to teach and reinforce the basics for posture, breath, and tone placement.

Alternating the exercises, and adding others to the ones presented here, will help to avoid the onset of routine boredom during the warm-up period, and will keep the rehearsal time fresh and interesting so that the singers will continue to pay attention to the various techniques employed and exercises being practiced.

C. PRE – SERVICE WARM – UP

Nowadays, many choirs gather together to do a warm-up immediately before a liturgical service. They will meet before a Vespers or a Divine Liturgy in a Church school classroom, the parish library, or in the large coffee hour room in the basement of the church building (if the choir meets for rehearsal on a Saturday afternoon before the Resurrectional Vespers, an added warm-up session is not necessary). This provides a double benefit for the singers: it gives them a chance to warm-up and stretch their vocal cords and breathing muscles before the service, and it also gives the choir director the opportunity to go over hymns that are specific to that particular liturgical service.

For example, if there is a given feast on a Sunday (say, Sunday of the Holy Cross during Great Lent, or Palm Sunday), the choir director will, at the pre-service warm-up, have the singers run through any special Antiphons, Troparia, Kontakia, special Trisagion, Prokeimena, Hymn to the Theotokos, and/or Communion Hymn that will be sung at that Divine Liturgy. Any musical trouble spots that were worked out at a previous rehearsal can be gone over again, to ensure that the singers have mastered the music at that point. Also, any places in the hymns where the wording of the liturgical text proved difficult can be sung through, to reinforce the clarity of the grammatical pronunciation on the part of the singers.

Usually, a pre-service warm-up is held a half-hour before the liturgical service begins. So, if the Sunday Divine Liturgy begins at 9 (or 9:30) am, the pre-service warm-up will commence at 8:30 (or 9) am, and conclude about ten to twelve minutes later. This gives the choir director a few minutes to go over the specifics to the reader who will be chanting the 3rd Hour that day, advising which troparia and kontakia will be done at the specific points in the Hour, which usually begins fifteen minutes before the beginning of the Divine Liturgy. This also has the added advantage of having all of the choir members present to listen to the 3rd Hour, which will further help them prepare themselves spiritually for singing during the liturgical service.

D. DICTION EXERCISES

In order for the singing to be understood so that, as St Paul said, "I will sing with the spirit, and I will sing with the mind, also." (1 Cor 14:15), the words of the hymns must be pronounced clearly and intelligently. To accomplish this, it is helpful to spend some rehearsal time on diction exercises. One good source for those is the set of exercises by Liz T., found on the Internet at http://takelessons.com/blog/ diction-exercises-z02. The following six exercises can prove to be most helpful in improving the diction of singers:

Tongue Twisters

Tongue twisters are good because they force a person to really focus on the pronunciation. A few helpful tongue twisters are:

- She sells seashells by the seashore.
- Red leather, yellow leather.
- Peter Piper picked a peck of pickled peppers.
- Who washed Washington's white woolen underwear, as Washington's washer woman went west?
- Mommy made me mash my M&M's.

Study Phonetics (IPA)

For this exercise, take a look at the song you're currently working on, and break down each word in the lyrics. Break apart the vowels, consonants, and diphthongs. Feel free to write in your score, if you need to spell a word differently for it to make sense in your singing.

Many singers refer to the IPA (**International Phonetic Alphabet) when singing. This** is a system derived from Latin that is used today as a standardized representation of sounds. It's a great tool for singers to use and study.

Practice Vowels

Take some time focusing on each of the vowels: ***ah***, ***ay***, ***ee***, ***oh***, and ***oo***. Add a consonant at the beginning (such as "mah, may, me…") and sing through the list, making sure each one is clear.

Practice Consonants

Next, focus on consonants, like *D*, *T*, and *N*. Practice speaking the different sounds, repeating each a few times.

Lip Buzz and Trill

Warm up your lips, tongue, and teeth with simple lip buzzes and tongue trills.

Breath Support

Pick one of the tongue twisters above, and practice saying it all in one breath.

Again, improving diction makes the meaning of the hymns more intelligible, easier to understand, and more prayerful.

8
LITURGICAL AWARENESS AND MUSICAL AWARENESS

Before articulating the specifics of how to rehearse the various hymns for the services, it is important to become conscious of two elements that you, as the choir director, will not only have to keep in mind throughout the rehearsal but that you will need to bring to the consciousness of your singers, as well. These two elements are liturgical awareness and musical awareness. Although each of these elements is a subtle one, the awareness of each will enable your choir members to sing in a manner that is prayerful and appropriate to the liturgical services.

A. LITURGICAL AWARENESS

Liturgical awareness refers to the function that a hymn has within a liturgical service, a feast, or an overall liturgical season. It therefore behooves the choir director to become familiar with the liturgical theology of the Orthodox Church, and there are numerous books that cover this in detail.[1] Acquisition of this knowledge will enable the director to interpret the musical element of the hymns in the appropriate liturgical perspective, and also allow him or her to conduct the singing of this hymnology in a manner that reflects the reality of the particular service, feast, or liturgical season.

For example, a hymn sung during the preparatory weeks of Great Lent and throughout that season is "Open to Me the Doors of Repentance" (although called for at the Resurrectional Matins service, it is often sung in many parishes during Resurrectional Vespers where the Matins service is not celebrated). The text of this hymn is as follows:

---

[1] Of particular importance and assistance are the works of Fr Alexander Schmemann. Cf., for example, his *For the Life of the World: Sacraments and Orthodoxy* (reprinted 2001), *Of Water and the Spirit: A Liturgical Study of Baptism* (1974), *Great Lent: Journey to Pascha* (revised edition 1974), and *The Eucharist: Sacrament of the Kingdom* (1987), all SVS (St Vladimir's Seminary) Press, Crestwood, NY.

Example 77

Glory to the Father, and to the Son, and to the
    Holy Spirit!
Open to me the doors of repentance,
    O Life – Giver,
for my spirit rises early to pray towards
    Your holy temple,
bearing the temple of my body all defiled!
But, in Your compassion, purify me by the
    loving – kindness of Your mercy!

Now and ever and unto ages of ages! Amen.
Lead me on the paths of salvation,
    O Mother of God,
for I have profaned my soul with shameful sins
and have wasted my life in laziness!
But, by your intercessions, deliver me from
    all impurity!

Have mercy on me, O God, according to
    Your great mercy,
and, according to the multitude of
    Your compassions,
blot out my transgressions!

When I think of the many evil things I have done,
wretch that I am,
I tremble at the fearful Day of Judgment!
But, trusting in Your loving – kindness,
like David, I cry to You:
"Have mercy on me, O God!
Have mercy on me, O God!
Have mercy on me, O God, according to
    Your great mercy!"

    Examining the text of this hymn, even without the music, it is apparent that the content of it is an acknowledgement of one's sinful inclinations and actions, and a desperate cry for help to God for repentance, healing, and salvation. This is a central theme of the entire season of Great Lent, especially the first half (the first three weeks).[2] Therefore, this hymn is *not* sung in a robust, festal manner, but somewhat slowly (without dragging!), softly, and penitentially.

    In contrast to this, the troparion of Pascha proclaims the central reality of our Orthodox Faith:

---

[2] Cf. Schmemann, Alexander, *Great Lent*, op. cit., pp. 76-77.

Example 78

**Christ is Risen from the dead,
trampling down death by death,
and, upon those in the tombs, bestowing life!**

Here, the content of the hymn is one of an absolute, final victory by God over the power of alienation, sin, and death. Therefore, this hymn is to be sung in the most joyous, victorious, and celebratory manner possible.

There are hymns that combine different elements within them and, so-to-speak, shift gears, perspective, or emphasis within them. Take, for example, the troparion for Palm Sunday:

Example 79

**By raising Lazarus from the dead before
   Your Passion,
You confirmed the universal resurrection,
   O Christ God!
Like the children with the palms of victory,
we cry out to You, O Vanquisher of death:
"Hosanna in the highest!
Blessed is He Who comes in the Name of the Lord!"**

This hymn, reflecting the events of Palm Sunday as recorded in the Gospels, illustrates the fact that the children (as well as the adults in the Gospel accounts) cried out and shouted victoriously the content of the last two lines of the hymn ("Hosanna in the highest! Blessed is He Who comes in the Name of the Lord!"). Therefore, an appropriate way to sing this hymn liturgically is to sing the first four lines (through "O Vanquisher of death") is a somewhat-soft-to-medium volume, and then, to manifest the acknowledgement of Christ as the Victorious One of God, to sing the last two lines ("Hosanna in the highest! Blessed is He Who comes in the Name of the Lord!") in a louder volume (without screaming) and in a robust, joyful, and celebratory manner. This is also the case with the second troparion for Palm Sunday:

Example 80

When we were buried with You in
    Baptism, O Christ God,
we were made worthy of eternal life by
    Your Resurrection!
Now, we praise You and sing:
"Hosanna in the highest!
Blessed is He Who comes in the Name of the Lord!"

Again, the first three lines (through "Now, we praise you and sing") are sung in a somewhat-soft-to-medium volume, and the last two lines ("Hosanna in the highest! Blessed is He Who comes in the Name of the Lord!") are sung in a louder volume (without screaming) and in a robust, joyful, and celebratory manner.

Another hymn that contains differing elements is from the Kanon of Holy Saturday (also sung at the Nocturns of Holy Saturday). Holy Saturday is a day of transition, placed between Holy Friday (the day of Christ's Passion and Crucifixion) and Holy Pascha (the day of Christ's Resurrection), the blessed Sabbath on which, as the hymns of the day proclaim, Christ experienced His own personal Sabbath by "resting" from all His works, lying dead in the tomb. The 9th ode of the Kanon clearly manifests the dual nature of this day:

Example 81

Do not lament me,
seeing Me in the tomb;
the Son conceived in the womb without seed!
For, I shall Arise
and be glorified with eternal glory as God!
I shall exalt all who magnify you in faith and in love!

The first three lines acknowledge the suffering of Christ's Passion and His Crucifixion on the Cross.

Beginning with the fourth line, however ("For, I shall Arise), this 9th ode anticipates the victorious Resurrection of Christ from the dead that follows His Crucifixion and blessed Sabbath in the tomb. Therefore, it is most appropriate to sing the first three lines (through "the Son conceived in the womb without seed") in a very soft volume, almost reflecting the silence of the Church and all of creation as they behold Christ hanging dead on the Cross, and then, beginning with the fourth line ("For, I shall Arise"), to sing it in a much louder volume through the remainder of the ode, majestically anticipating the victory about to be wrought on Holy Pascha with Christ's Resurrection from the dead!

Many other examples could suffice to reflect the liturgical realities and perspectives of different feasts. Celebrations such as Holy Theophany (Christ's Baptism in the Jordan and the manifestation of the Holy Trinity), Holy Pentecost (the descent of the Holy Spirit onto the Church), and Dormition (the falling asleep of the Theotokos and her entrance into Heaven, anticipating the general resurrection of all of us) are just some of the feasts that make present in the Church the saving work of our loving God in His victory over sin and death and our entrance into His eternal Kingdom.

B. MUSICAL AWARENESS

Musical awareness refers to the function of the musical elements within the hymnology of the liturgical services and their place and interaction within the various sections of the choir. Therefore, the choir director needs to be musically proficient as to how the voicings in the different parts function and how to best reflect that function in the singing of the hymnology.

A very common voice setting is found in the stikhera tones (familiar to most Orthodox as used for the stikhera on "Lord, I Call Upon You" and the Apostikha at Vespers) in the Russian Chant tradition. The following example is from tone 5:

Liturgical Awareness and Musical Awareness 153

Example 82

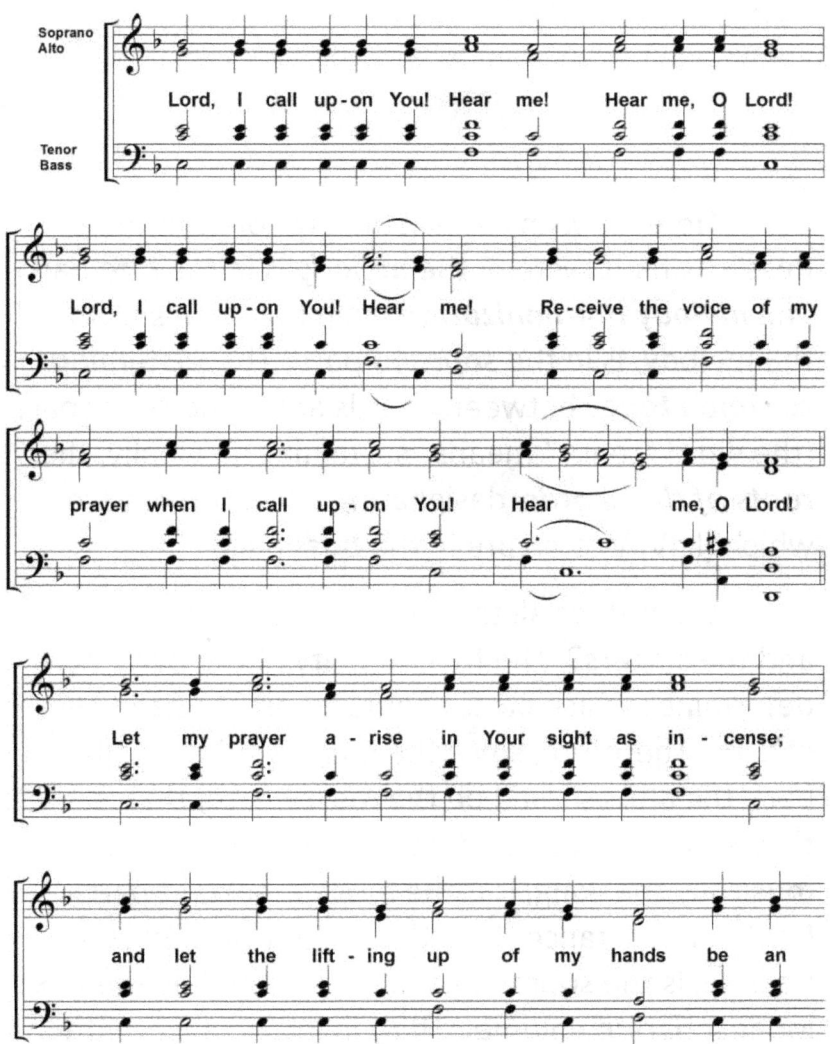

Here, as with all the stikhera tones in the Russian Chant system, the **melody** is in the **alto** part. The **melody harmonization**, up parallel 3rd's from the melody, is in the **soprano** part. The **sustaining common tones** between chords are in the **tenor** part (the word "tenor" means "sustaining"). Finally, the **roots of the chords**, designating which chords are which (I, IV, V, etc.) are in the **bass** part.

What does all this mean for the choir directors and the singers? The functionality of the parts here determines which parts should be emphasized over others. Therefore, since the melody is in the alto part, the altos should be the most heard, that is, they should be the loudest part in volume, since, musically speaking, it is the most important part. Next in importance, with the melody harmonization up a 3rd, is the soprano part. This should be the next loudest part in volume. Third in importance, with the roots of the chords determining the musical harmonization, is the bass part. The basses, then, should sing more softly than the altos and sopranos. Here, in the final place of importance with its use of the sustaining common tones, is the tenor part, which should be the softest in volume of the four parts. This does ***not*** mean that the bass and tenor parts should not be heard, or that the altos and sopranos should sing in an overly loud, blasting manner. It ***does*** mean that the choir director and all of the singers should be aware of the musical function of all four parts, and adjust the volume of each part accordingly to match and manifest those functions. In fact, a good rule of thumb for ***all*** singers should be this: If any singer cannot hear the singers in the other three parts, that singer is singing too loudly. So, even though the altos here should sing louder than the other sections, to bring out the main melody, they still need to sing in such a manner that each alto can hear the singing of the sopranos, the tenors, and the basses. Singers in the other three sections should sing accordingly, as well.

Another common voice setting in our Orthodox hymnology is the following:

Example 83

This is the Russian Chant setting for the Resurrectional Kontakion in tone 1 for the Sunday Divine Liturgy. Most of the Russian Chant troparion tones (used for the troparia and kontakia) have this particular voice setting. Here, we see that the **melody** is in the **soprano** part. The **melody harmonization**, again up parallel 3rd's from the melody itself, is in the **tenor** part. The **sustaining common tones** are here found in the **alto** part. And, once again, the **roots of the chords** are found in the **bass** part.

Again, the functionality of the parts determines the manner in which the hymn is sung. Therefore, since the sopranos have the melody here instead of the altos, the soprano part should be the loudest in volume. Next in both importance and volume should be the tenors, who have the melody harmonization. The basses, keeping their function of singing the roots of the chords, are again third in both importance and volume. Finally, with the singing of the sustaining common tones, the altos should be the softest in volume.

One final example should suffice for illustrating this concept of musical awareness. This is from the Georgian Chant setting of the Cherubic Hymn:

Example 84

In this particular voice setting, the **melody** is in the **alto** part. However, unlike the other examples we have looked at, there is **no** melody harmonization up in parallel 3rd's. Rather, **all three other parts** (soprano, tenor, and bass) just fill in the chord tones (root, 3rd, 5th) of the harmonization of this setting. Therefore, the altos, having the one and only melody, should be the loudest part in volume, with all three other parts (soprano, tenor, and bass) singing **much** softer than the altos, in order to bring the melody part to the forefront.

The knowledge of the functionality of the various parts of the four sections of the choir for the choir director, and the awareness of this functionality for all of the singers, will ensure that the singing of our Orthodox hymnology will be done in a manner that is appropriate to this functionality. The warm-up exercise in the previous chapter

(Example 72, on pages 126-127) is essential for bringing this awareness to the attention of all choir members. If, at any time, the singers become lax in their musical awareness, the practicing of this particular warm-up exercise will help remind and reinforce this musical awareness for everyone who is singing in our liturgical services.

9
REHEARSAL TECHNIQUES

Having articulated the elements of an opening prayer, warm-up exercises, liturgical awareness, and musical awareness, we are now ready to examine the particulars of the techniques used in a constructive choir rehearsal. While special circumstances will occur for each new hymn rehearsed, based on the musical particulars of that hymn, there are certain basic techniques that, when employed, result in a successful mastery of the musical elements involved, despite differences between musical settings.

A. INITIAL PREPARATION

Before singing any notes of a new arrangement of a hymn, it is helpful to go over the hymn from the viewpoints of liturgical awareness and musical awareness, as discussed in the previous chapter. So, for instance, looking at the Georgian Chant arrangement of the Cherubic Hymn that we looked at in chapter 8 (Example 84, pages 150-151), it is first suggested that the choir director discuss the place of the Cherubic Hymn in the Divine Liturgy, that it functions as the entrance hymn for the Eucharistic Entrance. Also worth mentioning is the fact that the two halves of the Cherubic Hymn are usually sung at a different tempo, the first half (through "all earthly cares") more slowly (to give the clergy time for their prayer, a small censing, the triple recitation of the Cherubic Hymn, and the preparation of the Holy Gifts on the Table of Oblation) and the second half (beginning with "Amen." and "That we may receive the King of all,...!") more briskly (since less time is required on the part of the clergy to place the Holy Gifts on the Altar Table, cense them, and then be ready to proceed with the following Litany of Supplication).

Another **very** good tool to use for liturgical awareness is, again before doing any singing, to read through the text of the hymn to be rehearsed. So many times, both choir directors and members sing the hymnology without paying any attention to the meaning of the text. In other words, they fail to **pray** with the hymns themselves. And, if the Church musicians sing without meaning, how can they hope to lead the rest of the congregation into praying with the hymnology? Look at the text of the Cherubic Hymn in the following example, which is free from any musical notation.

Example 85

Let us who mystically represent the Cherubim,
and who sing the thrice – holy hymn to the
    life – creating Trinity,
now lay aside all earthly cares!

Amen.
That we may receive the King of all,
Who comes invisibly upborne by
    the angelic hosts!
Alleluia! Alleluia! Alleluia!

Doesn't the meaning of the text stand out more clearly when free from the "distraction" of the musical elements? Again, reciting the hymnological texts out loud, without music, allows the meaning of the text to penetrate the minds and the hearts of the singers. And, if the choir members then begin singing with meaning, this will affect the style and manner of their singing, so that the rest of the people in the congregation (whether or not they sing along with the choir) will hear that meaning being carried through, and will then be able to pray with and enter into the meaning of the hymnological texts.

Staying with this Georgian Chant arrangement of the Cherubic Hymn, the choir director, after discussing the elements of liturgical awareness, can bring to the attention of the singers the elements of musical awareness that we discussed at the end of the previous chapter, namely, that the altos are the only section that sing the melody, that the other three sections (soprano, tenor, and bass) are basically singing chord tones and passing tones, so that the altos should be **the** prominent part heard in singing this arrangement and that, functioning as harmonic support, the other three sections should sing much more softly.

It is after discussing these liturgical and musical elements with the choir members that the choir director can now turn to the actual singing of the hymn.

B.   FIRST RUN - THROUGH

The choir director, be it a man or a woman, should begin by singing the melody part of the hymn (in his or her own comfortable range) all the way through, so the singers can hear the melody. Most choir members are not proficient at reading music and many do not read music at all, so that they tend to learn the music by rote. In singing this first run-through of the melody, it is advisable for the choir director to sing it at a slower pace than will actually be sung during the services. This gives the singers the chance to follow the music along on the page while simultaneously hearing the director sing their part. By going more slowly like this, the singers have a greater chance of hearing and remembering the notes and melody pattern so that, when they begin singing it for the first time, the possibility of them singing the right notes is maximized.

As mentioned, the choir director should sing the entire hymn all the way through the first time. Then, the director may, in singing it a second time, break the hymn down into smaller sections. For the sake of convenience, this arrangement is reprinted below.

Example 86

Rehearsal Techniques

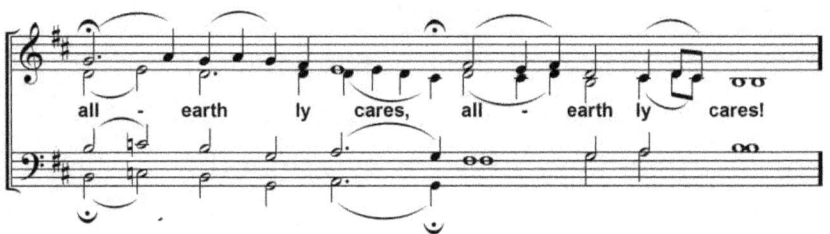

In singing the melody part for the alto section a second time, the director may want to sing only to the end of the first staff, concluding with the last syllable of "mystically". Then, the director should have the altos sing along with him or her (the director), and then have them sing the line by themselves, without the director singing. This leads to a gradual "independence" on the part of the singers: first, they have heard the director sing the line, followed by singing it along with the director, and finally singing it on their own. Any trouble spots or notes can be gone over and clarified by the choir director.

After singing the first line, the director can repeat this process with the second line (through the word "Cherubim"): the director should first sing it alone, then with the altos, and then have the altos sing it by themselves. Again, any trouble spots or notes can be gone over and clarified by the choir director. Once the second line has been sung successfully, the director should have the altos sing both lines together. If they do this smoothly the first time, then once is enough. If some of them still feel shaky about it, another repetition or two may prove helpful.

If you will notice while looking at this hymn, the first two lines contain the complete musical pattern for the entire hymn. The rest of the hymn is just the same melody pattern of the first two lines, repeated throughout. Therefore, once the altos have sung successfully through the first two lines, each of the other three parts may be added, one-by-one. In this case, it is best to next add the soprano part, since the tone quality is similar to the altos (both involve only women's voices) and the soprano part does have more moving notes than the tenors or the basses. Also, at times, the sopranos briefly move in parallel 3rd's to the altos (such as the beginning of the second line, on "rep" of "represent"), so the pairing of these two parts will reinforce one another. After this, the tenors can be added next, and, finally, the basses. When adding each of these three other parts, it would be helpful for the choir director to sing each part before having the sections themselves sing it. Since these three other parts are much simpler than the melody in the altos, the choir director can sing both first two lines together in demonstration before having the particular section join in. Again, if the director sings alone, then with the section, and finally has the section sing it by themselves, this will reinforce the musical pattern for that part.

As you go along as the choir director and rehearse each section's part, then add this to the parts previously rehearsed. So, as we said, once the sopranos learn their part, have them sing the first two lines together with the altos. Then, when the tenors have gotten their notes, have them sing together with both the altos and sopranos. Finally, when the basses master their part, have them sing together with the other three sections.

C. FINE TUNING

Once the various sections of the choir have pretty well mastered the notes in their respective parts of the hymn, you can concentrate on fine tuning the singing by concentrating on other elements. First of all, have your full choir sing together a few times, gradually building up the tempo from the slower, learning-the-notes pace to the actual tempo at which they will sing the hymn in the liturgical services.

Another important area to focus on is phrasing. Many choirs sing in a choppy manner, breathing in the middle of the line or textual phrase, thereby obscuring the meaning of the text. There are numerous settings of our hymnology in either fixed meter or in chant meter that still puts measure lines every so many notes along the way. Alert your singers to this situation, and make them aware to sing the hymn in complete thoughts and sentences. The previously-mentioned exercise of just speaking through the text, without music, is of great benefit here. If your singers are having a difficult time with the phrasing, go back to the speaking-the-text exercise and run through that a few times, having the choir members pay close attention to the textual phrasing.

Many modern composers and arrangers of liturgical music are aware of this particular problem, and are setting down the music of our hymnology accordingly. In this example of the Cherubic Hymn, notice that there are no bar lines or measure lines as such, but there *are* well-placed *phrase* lines. The first one occurs at the end of the second line, at the end of the word "Cherubim". The next one occurs at the end of the fourth line, at the end of the word "Trinity". And the third one occurs at the end of the sixth line, after the words "earthly cares". Advise your singers that these are the *only* places where everyone is to take a breath at the same time. At all other points in the singing, tell the choir members to practice what is called "staggered breathing", that is, each person is to take a breath where they comfortably need to, staggering these breath points with the other singers so that the smooth flow of the textual phrase is not hampered and the singing becomes choppy. Again, with other settings that include many bar or measure lines, more careful attention will need to be paid to this aspect of the singing.

    Along with tempo and phrasing, careful time and attention will need to be given to balance and blend. The musical awareness on the part of the choir members will prove helpful here. Keeping the functionality of the various parts in mind will allow the singers to adjust their volume to provide the right balance to let the melodic lines sound forth. As previously mentioned, with this particular arrangement, the altos, having the one and only melody part, need to be heard above everyone else. The remaining three parts, filling in the chord notes and passing tones, need to sing much more softly. This is what is meant by the term "balance".

The term "blend" refers to the ability of all the choir members to sing in such a manner that it sounds like one voice doing the singing. Careful attention needs to be paid in rehearsals to ensure that the singers all come in together on the first note, end together on the cadence cut-off's, and blend together throughout the rest of the phrases. Here, again, the choir members need to listen to each other and to the other sections of the choir as they sing the hymns. Watching the choir director is imperative. If you find your singers are not watching well and have troubling blending, have them close their music binders and try singing portions of the hymns from memory, paying attention and watching the choir director intently so as to sing as one unit. Periodic reminders and closed-book practicing will result in better blending on the part of the singers.

As you become more proficient as a choir director, you will naturally find yourself using expressive gestures to enhance the liturgical singing. In the Cherubic Hymn cited here, many choirs have found it to be a natural inclination to gradually sing louder (crescendo) at the beginning of the second line (on the word "represent"), then to gradually soften the volume (decrescendo) at the end of the phrase (on the words "the Cherubim"). A heightened sense of both liturgical awareness and musical awareness, working together, will enable the director to develop a liturgical "sixth sense", so to speak, so that he or she will instinctively know how to direct a particular hymn more expressively, to bring out the meaning of the text. This skill is developed gradually over the years, as one gains more experience directing the music during the various services.

D. POSITIVE REINFORCEMENT

Two other elements are necessary for the successful mastery of music at the choir rehearsal. The first of these is positive reinforcement. As any teacher will tell you (and, in the context of the rehearsal, the choir director **does** function as a teacher), those who are learning, be they students in a school or singers in a choir, are still human beings with the accompanying frailties and emotions that we all have. As such, when trying to master new skills or acquire new knowledge, much hard work and effort is required to accomplish this task. This can prove to be very demanding, both physically and emotionally. Using positive reinforcement to encourage and guide your singers is absolutely essential. When working with a section on a difficult passage, as your singers gradually master the notes and expressive elements of the hymnology, all along the way the director should make short little comments, such as, "Good!", "Better!", "That's it!", "Now you've got it!", "Great!", etc. Along with helping to keep a casual, light, easy-going atmosphere to the rehearsal, positive reinforcement also serves as necessary feedback to let the choir members know when they are on the right track in learning the music.

    Another element in keeping a light tone to the rehearsal is to use a sense of humor. Care needs to be taken to make sure that any humorous remarks are both appropriate and applicable to the situation. To cite an example, whenever the singers in my choir began to forget to use good posture and proper breath support, resulting in a flattening of the notes of the hymn, I would remind them that, if they watched me, the director, intently, they would see that I was standing with good posture and was also periodically gesturing towards my abdomen to remind them of proper breath support. Watching me in that manner would therefore help them to stand properly, breathe correctly, and keep the pitch up. I would then end this explanation by saying, "In other words, if you see sharp (**C$^\#$**), you won't be flat (**B^b**)!" This would be followed by some light laughter on the part of the singers. Yet, using humor in this manner of it being a teaching tool is very effective. The choir members, in remembering the humorous phrase, would tend to retain for a longer time the awareness of the need for good posture and proper breath support. Again, this element needs to be used sparingly, in order for the rehearsal not to devolve into a stand-up act in a comedy club. However, periodic use of humor as a teaching tool for difficult musical passages can prove to be very helpful.

E. PHRASING

Another **very** important aspect of Orthodox liturgical singing that needs to be extensively dealt with in rehearsals is the concept of phrasing. What is absolutely **essential** in the celebration of our services is that the content of the hymnody, the text, is ***prayerfully intelligible***. That is, the meaning of the text needs to make sense so that the people may interiorize it and liturgically celebrate it in a prayerful manner. Alas, too often this is the liturgical component that is overlooked and slips through the cracks, so to speak.[1]

The following example is one that can be used to illustrate this point.

---

[1] I am grateful to Nadia Koblosh, to whom this book is dedicated, for making me aware of the importance of phrasing. She is the first choir director I ever saw who rehearsed her singers to phrase properly.

Example 87

This is the tone 8 setting of the Russian Chant melody for "Lord, I Call Upon You" at Vespers. In this specific example, the bar lines provided do *not* function as measure lines, but as ***phrase*** lines. Therefore, the singers should all take a breath at the following points: after the first instance of the word "me"; after the second instance of the word "Lord"; after the third instance of the word "me"; after the third instance of the word "You"; and, after the last instance of the word "Lord". These are the **only** places that all the singers should **collectively** breathe together (singers who need to breathe elsewhere can do so individually on their own). However, the singers in **many** choirs have gotten into the habit of taking a breath or a break after each elongated note (half notes and whole notes). In this hymn, for example, the singers would, with**out** conscious focus and rehearsal on the part of the choir director, tend to take a breath or a break after the word "prayer," which is on a half note. This would result in the fragmenting of the meaning of the text. While it is true that the first part of this phrase, "Receive the voice of my prayer," could stand independently on its own, the same can**not** be said of the second part of the phrase, "when I call upon You." This, in and by itself, is an *in*complete thought, leading one to ask the question, "**What about** 'when I call upon You'?" The answer is found in the **complete** phrase, "**Receive the voice of my prayer** when I call upon You!"

Another classic example of this is found in the Beatitudes, which are sung as the Third Antiphon at most Divine Liturgies of the year. Again, the following example utilizes bar lines that function as **phrase** lines:

Example 88

As can be readily seen, if the singers, by force of habit, take a breath or a break at every half note in the middle of the phrases, each second-half-of-a-phrase will present an *in*complete and ***fragmented*** thought: "when You come in Your Kingdom!"; "for theirs is the Kingdom of Heaven!"; "for they shall be comforted!"; etc. **Only** when the words and syllables occurring on the half notes at the end of the first half of the phrases ("remember us, O Lord"; "poor in spirit"; "those who mourn"; etc.) are **connected** to the second half of each phrase does the **whole** phrase/sentence/thought make sense.

This is a **vital** and **essential** element of our liturgical singing. It is imperative that all choir directors become acutely aware of the content of **complete** phrases in our hymnology, and accordingly rehearse the singers to sing that hymnology in **complete** thoughts and sentences.

F. WOODSHEDDING

The term "woodshedding" refers to the practice of breaking down difficult musical passages into workable units of notes so that each unit of only a few notes can be focused on and mastered. As a person may take a piece of wood and, using a knife, whittle away at the wood until it is shaped into an object (a flute, a pen, etc.), so the singers focus on these small units of notes in order to "whittle" away the difficulty in mastering these notes. Then, as each group is mastered, it is then paired again with the other units of notes around it until the musical phrase is sung successfully in its entirety.

Returning again to the Georgian Chant arrangement of the Cherubic Hymn, we notice a rhythmically difficult section on the second line, in the alto and soprano parts, on the last syllable of "represent", reproduced below.

Example 89

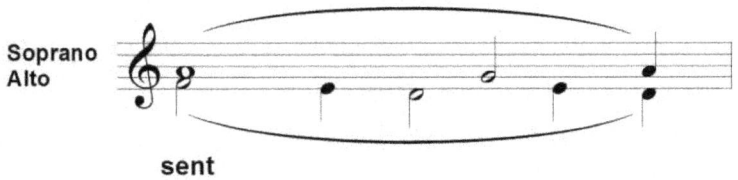

Here, there is an interchange of note movement between the two voices. After the altos move down to the first **D**, the sopranos move down to the **G** on the very next beat. On the beat immediately following this, the altos move back up to the **E**, and then both voices move to their respective last notes of the syllable (altos to the *D*, sopranos to the *A*) at the same time. At first, this alternating note movement between the two parts in this rhythm can be confusing, and many choir members from one section may be tempted to move at the same time as the singers in the other section. There are a couple of ways to woodshed this section. One is for the choir director to sing each part (alto, soprano) in turn, clapping a quarter-note rhythm out while singing the part. Then, have the choir members of that section sing their part, while either clapping the quarter-note rhythm with you or tapping their foot to it. Do this a few times so that the singers get the feel of how many beats are on each note value. Then, when you put the two parts together, to be sung at the same time, cue each section (alto and soprano) when they move to their next note. For instance, the director will point to the altos when they move down, both from the $F^\#$ to the first *E*, and then again from this first *E* to the *D*; then, on the next beat, the director points to the sopranos to move down from the first *A* to the *G*; then, on the next beat, the director points to the altos to move from the *D* to the second *E*; finally, the director points to both sections to move to their final notes (*D* for the altos, *A* for the sopranos). Practice this small musical unit slowly and repeatedly (three to five times), while pointing to the sections for their respective note movements. Then, have the sections sing this unit two or three times with**out** pointing to the sections, to see if the singers have internalized the rhythm of the unit. When this is accomplished and the two parts have mastered the rhythm, then have all four parts sing the complete phrase (the first two lines, through the word "Cherubim") and see if the rhythm mastery still holds up. If so, sing the complete phrase another one or two times, to emphasize and confirm the rhythm mastery on the part of the singers.

This is the essence of woodshedding, to break problematic areas down to the isolated notes in question, rehearsing them correctly quite a few times to master the particular musical problem in the small unit, and then to regroup the small unit back to the larger phrase unit once again. Since this is such a key and vital aspect of the rehearsal, we will present some more examples to illustrate this concept.

For various feasts of the Theotokos (such as her Entrance into the Temple on 21 November), there is a Kievan Chant setting of the tone 3 Prokeimenon for the feast, shown as follows:

Example 90

One possibly troublesome area in this arrangement, note-wise, is in the bass part, with the ascending run from the lower **D** to the upper **D**, on the words "rejoices in God". This isolated section can be viewed as follows:

Example 91

Here, the basses move up the scale step-wise, from **D** to **E** to **F**#. Then, the movement switches from step-wise to chordal; in other words, the notes now reflect a **D** major triad, going from the **F**# to the **A** to the upper **D**. An effective way to woodshed this is, first of all, to have the basses sing the notes on a ***non***-solfege syllable, such as "doo". This will free the singers from having to concentrate on both notes and text at the same time, leaving their full attention on just learning the notes. Sing the note progression (lower **D, E, F**#**, A,** upper **D**) slowly, one note at a time, ***pausing*** for two or three seconds to sustain the singing of each note. Do this two or three times. Then, have the basses sing along with you, the choir director, ***again*** pausing for two or three seconds on each note. Then, increase the tempo **slightly** from the original pausing tempo, and repeat this two or three times. Continue this procedure, **gradually** increasing the tempo, repeating the exercise each two or three times, until the correct tempo is reached. When it is, and the singers can sing the notes correctly on the given tempo, **then** have them sing this unit with the words of the text ("rejoices in God") matched back with the notes. Do this two or three times to reinforce the correct notes with the text. When this is successfully accomplished, have the basses sing their part of the Prokeimenon completely, from beginning to end ("My soul magnifies the Lord, and my spirit rejoices in God, my Savior!"). Again, do this two or three times. When this is done, bring in the other three parts and have the entire choir sing the Prokeimenon through twice completely; then, the third time, have them sing the last half of the Prokeimenon ("and my spirit rejoices in God, my Savior!"), as they will do during the Divine Liturgy for the feast. If, in woodshedding this section, you find that the basses are having difficulty with the notes in the descending run (on the words, "God, my Savior!"), isolate this small musical unit, rehearse it as you did with the ascending run on "rejoices in God", and then put it together with the entire Prokeimenon, as before.

You will notice that each step in the procedure of woodshedding this small musical unit is to be repeated two or three times. This is a **vital** element in the woodshedding and learning process. Many choir directors make the mistake of waiting until the choir members sing the notes correctly only once, and then they stop the procedure, moving on quickly to something else. What they don't realize is that this first time correctly singing the notes is only the **beginning**: they have sung the passage *in*correctly multiple times before, but have only sung it **once** correctly! This one-time (maybe by chance or by luck) correct rendition of the notes needs to be reinforced again and again, until the correct notes become a part of the singers' tonal memory. The reason many directors fail to repeat and reinforce the correct singing is that they figure the singers will become bored, or that it will take too much rehearsal time to go over the passage again. First of all, working at and finally getting the correct notes is **not** boring to any singer who seriously wishes to learn the music and take their ministry seriously. Secondly, not reinforcing the correct version, letting it slip back to the wrong way of singing the passage, and then having to come back and woodshed it all over again, actually wastes **more** time than if, once the correct notes have been sung, they are reinforced immediately. Thirdly and finally, if the choir director goes through the woodshedding process in a relaxed but efficient manner, a small passage like this can be sung through five times within a regular 60-second minute. After each correct repetition, use positive reinforcement for encouragement before the next repetition, saying things like, "Better! Let's try it again!" and "Great! Let's do it once more to be sure that we have it down correctly!". If you will couple a relaxed atmosphere with a quickly-moving-forward, efficient repetition of the small musical units and positive reinforcement in between each repetition, you will amaze yourself at how much good work you can accomplish in just a five-minute period of your rehearsal. And, remember: if your rehearsal is an hour-and-a-half to two hours, this five-minute period is a very small percentage of the total rehearsal time. This small investment of time taken to learn difficult passages and repeating and reinforcing the correct singing, once it has been accomplished, will reap big dividends in the learning of new music and arrangements for your choir.

How does one go about rehearsing a hymn of epic size and proportion? Let us do a detailed analysis of rehearsing two major hymns, first the Sergei Rachmaninoff arrangement of "Rejoice, O

Virgin Theotokos" and then the Nikolai Rimsky-Korsakov arrangement of the Communion Hymn.

Example 92

This hymn, so classic and so beautiful, contains significant movement and melodic elements in each of the four parts. Its very expressive use of volume, crescendos, decrescendos, and harmonic chord progressions, make it a very prayerful arrangement when it is sung properly. Being a long piece, we will show it and rehearse it in sections.

In the beginning, at first glance, it seems the altos have the melody with the sopranos having a melody harmonization up in parallel 3rd's. Looking more closely, however, at the beginning of the second line, it looks like the **sopranos** have the melody with the tenors having the melody harmonization up in parallel 3rd's. Therefore, the first line has the **sopranos** with the main melody, and the **altos** with the melody harmonization **down** in parallel 3rd's. The assigning of melody functionality in such a simplistic manner, though, cannot be held to strictly, because the melodic kernels seem to switch voices frequently. For example, on line 2, on the word "grace", the lower three voices (alto, tenor, and bass) contain the descending quarter-and-eighth-note kernel, with the sopranos in a supportive function on the half note before the eighth-note movement. Then, on the words "the Lord is with you", the two melodicallymoving lines shift back to the altos and sopranos. It is important that the choir director, before having the choir members sing one note of this hymn, explain this shifting of function and melodic voicing to the singers, to make them musically aware of when they should bring their parts out more by singing louder and when they should pull back by singing softer. For instance, on the second line, the sopranos would sing "Mary, full of" (where they have key melodic movement) more loudly, pull back on "grace" (with the basic sustaining function of the half note), and then sing more loudly on their resumed melodic movement on "the Lord is with you". The altos, having a supporting function on "Mary, full of", would sing somewhat softly here, but then, with important melodic movement both on "grace" and "the Lord is with you", would sing louder for the rest of the phrase. The tenors have melodic movement on "Mary, full of" and "grace", and so should sing out more there, without overpowering the women's voices. However, even though they have some movement on "the Lord is with you", you can tell by the notes that, rather than a melody line, the tenors function here in filling in chord tones, so they should pull back on this section. The basses have chord tone function on "Mary, full of" and "the Lord is with you", and should sing softly in those places. Only on the word "grace" do the basses reflect melodic movement that parallels the altos and tenors, so only there should they increase their volume slightly before pulling back for the rest of the phrase. Again, it is imperative that the choir director explain these subtle changes in musical function in minute detail to the singers, in order for the choir members to mark their music accordingly (having pencils and erasers conveniently handy at choir rehearsals is a must!), to aid them in the coming forward and pulling back that is dependent on their musical function at any given time. Once this musical awareness has been explained, **then** the singers are ready for their first run-through on these first two lines. A final reminder to **all** of the singers is that this first section is sung softly (**p**) to very softly (**pp**). Once they have sung this first phrase a few times and gotten the correct notes, have them sing it again, keeping one eye on you, the choir director, so they can follow your direction for crescendos, decrescendos, and any other expressive gestures that are appropriate to the singing of this hymn.

The next section completes the "Mary, full of grace" portion and begins a new section.

Example 93

Again, each of these sections, as presented here, should be rehearsed as sub-divided units, to enable the singers to master the large musical material of this hymn in doable sections. At the beginning of the first line of this section, the altos have the main melodic material, paralleled by the basses, on "Mary, full of". On the word "grace", this double melodic function switches to the altos and the tenors. On "the Lord is with you", it further switches to the altos and the sopranos. At each of these points, only the two particular voices with the main melodic movement should be stressed.

On the second line, the basses are totally silent. Actually, this next section really starts at the end of the first line, where the altos are split into parallel 3rd's in singing the text, "Blessed are you among women and blessed is the Fruit of your womb!" (the latter part of which is continued in the next section). A polyphonic situation occurs here because, while the altos are singing this, the sopranos and tenors are singing, in unison (or octaves, actually) another melody on another text, "Virgin Theotokos, Mary, full of grace, the Lord is with you!". Since the singing of this is stressed by both the doubling of the voices (soprano and tenor) and the tone quality of the voices (sopranos are the high women's voices; tenors are the high men's voices), it would be **very** easy for these two voices to end up drowning out the other key melody and text being sung by the altos. Therefore, it is best to have the sopranos and tenors sing at this ***pianissimo*** (***pp*** [very soft]), while the altos sang either *piano* (*p* [soft]) or even *mezzo piano* (*mp* [medium soft]).

Example 94

This polyphonic situation, with one melody-and-text in the altos and the other in both the sopranos and the tenors, continues through most of the first line presented here. Again, even though all three voices call for *piano* (*p* [soft]), I would keep that designation for the sopranos and tenors, while allowing the altos to increase to either *mezzo piano* (*mp* [medium soft]) or even *mezzo forte* (*mf* [medium loud]), to balance out the voices as previously mentioned.

At the end of the first line (on, "For you have Borne the Savior of our souls!"), everyone is on the volume level *fortissimo* (*ff* [very loud]). Care needs to be taken here, however, so that the increased volume does not lead to a shouting-like quality in the singing. Beginning here, at the end of the first line, and continuing through the first half of the second line, the basses and altos are in unison in singing, "For, you have Borne the Savior", while the soprano and tenor parts are each split in parallel 3rd's, singing, "the Lord is with you!".

At the end of the second line, the basses are still singing with the altos on "you have Borne the Savior", with the altos having the more intricate melodic movement on the eighth notes, in contrast to the basses' quarter-note movement. The sopranos and tenors continue together on "Borne the Savior", with the sopranos clearly having a supporting function to the tenors' more melodic movement.

Example 95

In this section, in the first part of the first line, the tenors have the most active melodic movement of all four parts, repeating the entire phrase, "You have Borne the Savior!", in their eighth-note melody. The other three parts sing a melisma on the word, "Savior!", the alto and bass lines more active than the sopranos, who stay on a sustained **C**.

Beginning at the end of the first line and concluding through the end of the hymn, all four parts are textually together on "Borne the Savior of our souls!". The sopranos clearly have the melody here, with active support from the other three parts. As though there weren't enough variety in this exquisitely-composed hymn already, Rachmaninoff gives us one last bit of it at the end, with the suspended notes on "of" in the tenors and basses before resolving on the delayed "our". This needs to be emphasized without hitting the notes too harshly.

Once the various sections of the hymn have been rehearsed, the entire piece can now be gone through. The following is the rendering of the complete hymn.

Example 96

Rehearsal Techniques

Again, gradually rehearsing this hymn in sections as presented in Examples 90-93 will allow the singers to successfully accomplish mastery of the musical elements involved without getting over-taxed or too easily tired of this hymn. Taking 20 to 30 minutes to work out each section at a rehearsal, then setting it aside to rehearse other hymns, will keep the singing of this hymn new and fresh for all of your choir members. Woodshedding the various sections, little by little and week by week, will eventually result in a prayerful rendition of this hymn by your parish choir.

Finally, let us look at the Rimsky-Korsakov arrangement of the Communion Hymn. The first couple of phrases are as follows:

Example 97

Again, as with the other hymns we have looked at, the choir director would sing the parts for the various sections individually, then have the singers from each section sing it with you (the director), and then finally sing it themselves. Here, it would be best to take just the first phrase, with only the sopranos and altos, that goes to the middle of the second staff system. (**Note:** For smoothness of singing, it is best to conduct this hymn as though it were in "cut time", that is, with the half note equaling one beat.) Begin with the soprano part and go through the three-fold singing process (director alone, director with the section members, the section members on their own). Then, repeat this three-fold singing process with the alto part. After this, have both parts sing together, advising the altos that you (the director) will cue them for when they come in after the first four beats (they, the altos, come in on the word "praise" when the sopranos come in on the word "Lord") and advising the sopranos that the text for their notes is above the staff. Go over this two or three times with both sections. If either section gets off-track or confused about their part, rehearse it with that section in isolation, singing it by themselves a few times until they are very comfortable with it, then joining it together again with the part of the other section.

The next phrase comprises the last half of the second staff system and all of the third one. Once again, begin with the soprano part, stressing the importance of the rhythm and that, at the beginning of this second phrase, the sopranos stay on the word "praise" for the equivalent of three half-note beats before moving to the word "the". The same thing applies to them on the third staff system: They stay on the word "Lord" for three half-note beats before moving to the word "from". After the sopranos are comfortable with their part, rehearse the altos for their part, pointing out to them that, in this second phrase, they come in at the beginning of the phrase with the sopranos, but that they move through the words of the text ("Praise the Lord") sooner than the sopranos do. Once the altos are confident of their part, have them sing it together with the soprano part a few times.

Then, rehearse the tenor part, advising them that they come in at the beginning of the third half-note beat. Once they have their part down, put it together with the sopranos and altos, advising the tenors that you, the director, will cue them in for their entrance. Go over these three parts together a few times until all three sections are comfortable with this. Then, rehearse the bass part, having them repeat it until they are confident with it. Before pairing them up with the other three sections, advise the basses that they come in on the fifth half-note beat, and that you will cue them in for their entrance. Repeat this second phrase a few times, until the singers from all four sections feel comfortable with both their respective parts and where their entrances occur. Once this is done, then put both phrases together, having all the singers sing these first two phrases that comprise the first three staff systems.

At this point, take a break from rehearsing this hymn. If everything up to this point has been done, you and your singers will have accomplished a great deal in this one session. Trying to do any more on it at this point will tire the singers out. It would be best to come back to this hymn at another rehearsal, when the singers are more refreshed.

During that subsequent rehearsal, have all four parts sing these first two phrases together a couple of times, to review and confirm what was accomplished at the previous rehearsal. Then, take up the next section of the hymn, as follows:

Example 98

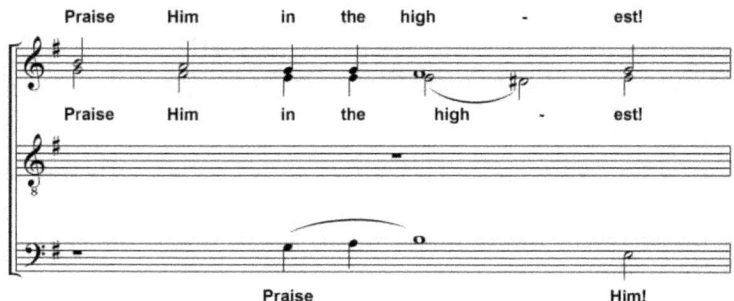

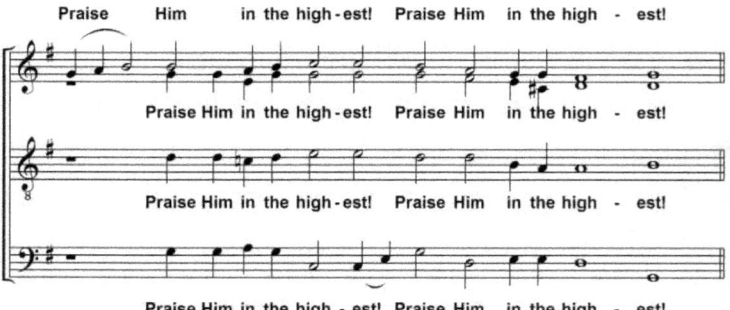

Here, begin with just the first line. Again, rehearse the soprano and alto parts separately, then together. Then, go over the bass part with that section, reminding them that they will come in on the third half-note beat, and that you will cue them in. Once they are comfortable with their part, put it together with the sopranos and altos. As can be seen, the tenors are silent on this line.

On the next line, the last before the "Alleluia!", the sopranos come in from the very beginning, with the other three parts all coming in on the third half-note beat. As before, rehearse the sopranos alone, then the altos alone, then the sopranos and altos together. After this, rehearse the tenors alone, then put them together with the sopranos and altos a couple of times. Finally, rehearse the basses alone, then all three parts.

The last line, the first one with the "Alleluia!", is similar to the very first line at the beginning of the hymn. Again, rehearse the sopranos alone, then the altos alone, then the sopranos and altos together. Finally, run through all three lines that were gone over today a couple of times.

At the third rehearsal, begin with a review:

Example 99

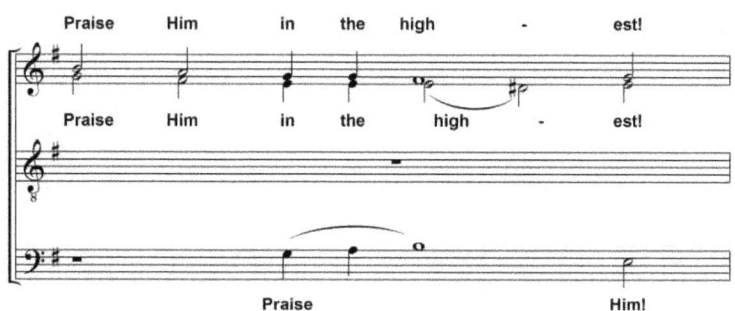

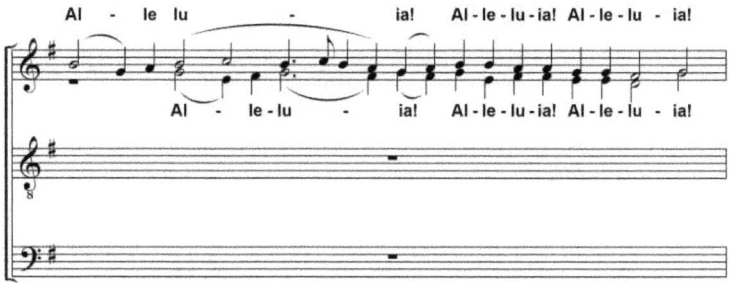

Since this encompasses a large portion of the hymn, go over this section twice before moving on to the last portion of the hymn, which is as follows:

Example 100

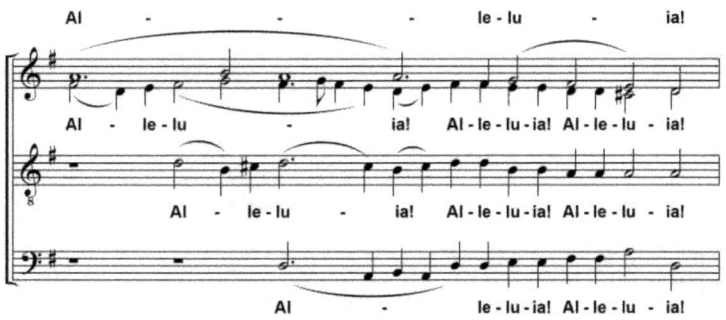

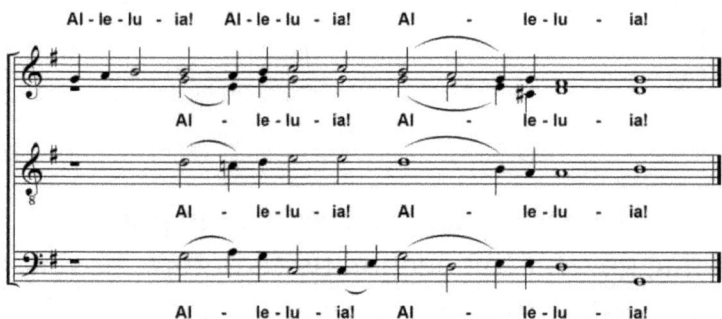

Again, this final section is parallel to the final section of the "Praise the Lord" portion of the hymn. Show that similarity to your singers, reminding them of the same details here that you did for the earlier section. For example, the sopranos here again have a dotted whole note (equal to three half-note beats) followed by a half note, followed by another dotted whole note. As before, rehearse each staff system separately. So, focusing just on the first staff system, rehearse the sopranos alone, then the altos alone, then both sopranos and altos together. Follow this with the tenors alone, reminding them that you will cue them in for their entrance on the third half-note beat, then pairing the tenors together a couple of times with the sopranos and altos. Finally, work with the basses alone, reminding them that you will cue them in for their entrance on the fifth half-note beat, then pairing them up a couple of times with the other three parts.

For the second staff system, where the tenors are again silent, rehearse the sopranos alone, the altos alone, the sopranos and altos together, the basses alone, and finally the sopranos, altos, and basses all together.

For the third and final staff system of the hymn, show the singers that the sopranos begin right away, with all three other parts coming in on the third half note beat. Rehearse the parts for this final line as follows: Sopranos alone, altos alone, sopranos and altos together, tenors alone, tenors with sopranos and altos, basses alone, basses with all three other parts.

When completed, first congratulate your singers for accomplishing a major volume of work, and then run through the entire hymn, from start to finish, a couple of times as follows:

Example 101

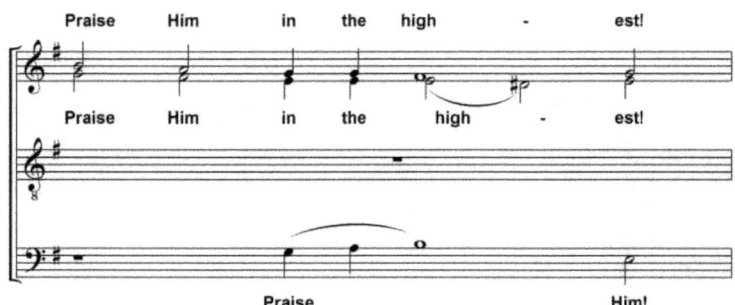
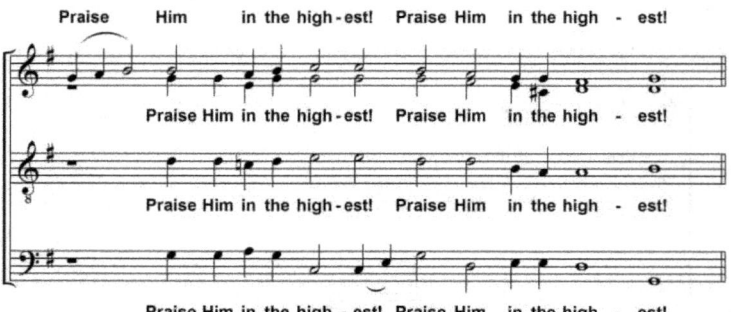

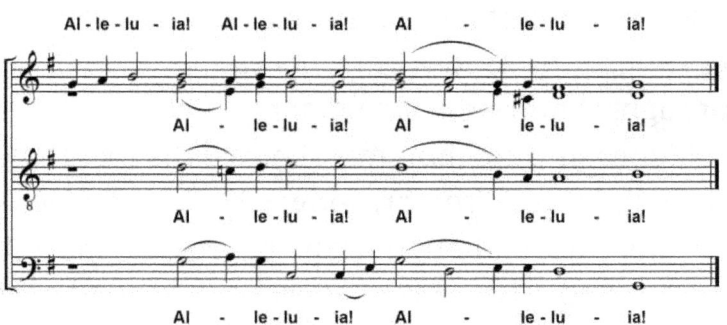

At the next two rehearsals, to reinforce and confirm all that the singers have accomplished, run through the entire hymn, from beginning to end, two or three times. Again, if the run-through is successful, give praise and positive feedback to your singers for working through such a lengthy hymn and learning it so well.

As you can see, the successful rehearsing of any of our Orthodox hymnology is dependent upon a thorough study and mastery of the musical elements on the part of the choir director **beforehand**, before you even think of presenting it to your choir. Introducing new music to your choir that you are unfamiliar with yourself will result in a quick awareness of that situation on the part of your singers, plus a growing mistrust as to the quality of the use of your rehearsal time. Knowing the music inside and out beforehand, however, and then presenting it to your singers in a confident and thoroughly knowledgeable manner, will instill confidence in your choir members of the fact that you, as the choir director, know what you are doing, will instill trust in them that the rehearsal time will be put to good use, and will encourage them to look forward to choir rehearsals as a time to further engage themselves in this joyful ministry of Orthodox liturgical singing.

Rehearsal Techniques 219

It may be fitting to conclude all your choir rehearsals with the Hymn to the Theotokos, as follows:

Example 102

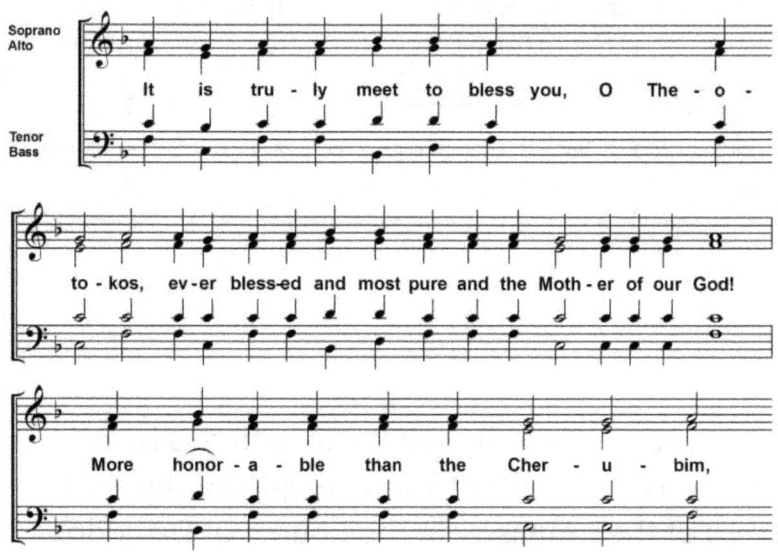

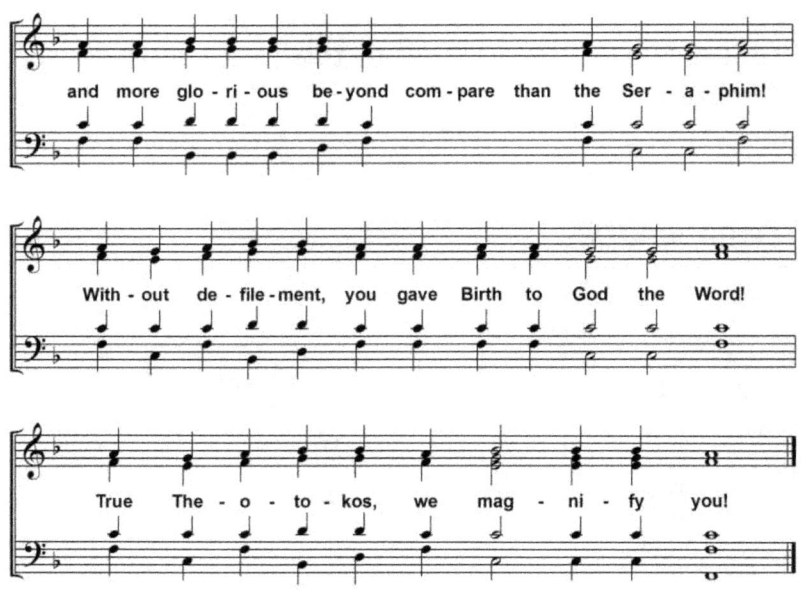

Concluding the rehearsal with this hymn serves as a reminder to your singers of the spiritual basis of their ministry in the Church of Orthodox liturgical music.

10
LITURGICAL TEAMWORK

One final subject that needs to be addressed in regards to the ministry of conducting and rehearsing Orthodox liturgical music is the extremely vital relationship between the choir director and the main celebrant of the liturgical services. Though, at times, this may be the diocesan bishop or the Metropolitan (usually during a pastoral visit, the dedication of a church building, or a significant parish anniversary), most of the time this refers to the priest who is the pastor of that particular parish (the other exception may be a priest who is filling in for the pastor who is away on vacation or ill). Since the liturgical singing comprises an average of 75% of the services (more during the Pascha season, less during Great Lent), the coordination and cooperation between these two people has great influence and lasting repercussions on the life of the parish community.

A. "... DECENTLY AND IN ORDER!"

The foundational basis for the relationship between the choir director and the main celebrant is given to us scripturally by St Paul:

> "But, all things should be done decently and in order!" (1 Corinthians 14:40).

Here, we have the fundamental reference for **all** ministries within the Church: everything, whether it be celebrating the liturgical services, education, mission, outreach, giving alms, or whatever, needs to be done in a manner that reflects the peace of Christ (Who *is* our Peace!) and the "righteousness and peace and joy in the Holy Spirit!" (Romans 14:17). This is further reflected in the fruit of the Holy Spirit, as enumerated by St Paul:

"But, the fruit of the Spirit is love, joy, peace, patience, kindness, goodness, faithfulness, gentleness, self-control!" (Galatians 5:22).

With this as the "canon", the measuring stick and reference point, both the choir director and the main celebrant can work together in a loving and harmonious manner, to work out the details of the liturgical services so that the flow of these very services goes along smoothly and efficiently.

B. THE MAIN CELEBRANT AS THE REFERENCE POINT

With this in mind, even though it is not an official canon of the Orthodox Church, it has been the practice within the Holy Tradition down through the centuries that the main celebrant is the reference point for all decisions and details concerning the celebration of the liturgical services. Again, most of the time, this main celebrant will be the priest who is the pastor of the local parish. However, if the diocesan bishop is presiding, he, then, becomes the main celebrant and makes the final decisions regarding liturgical details. If, furthermore, the Metropolitan is present to preside, then he supercedes the authority of both the parish priest and the diocesan bishop. Thus, by acknowledging and respecting each person in his or her position of function of ministry within the Church, the celebration of the liturgical services done in a manner "decently and in order" is ensured. Everyone needs to embrace the humility to acquiesce to the next person in the hierarchy of ministries. This applies as equally to the parish priest (when the diocesan bishop is present) and to the diocesan bishop (when the Metropolitan is present) as it does to the choir director.

C. THE LITURGICAL BLESSING

As an acknowledgement of this reality of the main celebrant as the liturgical reference point, it has started becoming the practice in some parishes for the choir director, before the liturgical service begins, to approach the main celebrant and receive a liturgical blessing to direct the choir and (by extension) the entire liturgical community in the musical responses. This is a good practice that, hopefully, will extend to more and more parishes. The reason for such is the following: All of the liturgical celebrants within the sanctuary, whether they be the deacon(s), the altar servers, the priest(s) (if there be a bishop or Metropolitan presiding), need to approach the main celebrant for a blessing to serve in the sanctuary. Throughout the service itself, a deacon (if there be any serving) will, at different times, bow to the priest as he goes to exit the sanctuary to chant the next litany. If there is a bishop or Metropolitan presiding, any of the priests serving will bow and receive a blessing from the bishop to chant the following prayer or exclamation. If, then, it is important for these celebrants to manifest the humility and obedience due to the main celebrant throughout the services, is it not important, also, for the choir director, who (as we have stated) will be directing about 75% of the liturgical activity, to also manifest his or her humility and obedience by asking for a similar blessing from the main celebrant? This brings about positive results on a couple of levels. First of all, it is a daily reminder to the choir director, when he or she receives the liturgical blessing, to work together with the main celebrant in humility and obedience, so that the services flow smoothly with all those actively involved in celebrating the services knowing what will occur and everyone being, so to speak, "on the same page". Secondly, there are some clergy (priests and bishops) who, not having musical knowledge or proficiency, feel uncomfortable or distrustful when relating with the choir director. By submitting himself or herself in humility and obedience to the main celebrant through the receiving of the liturgical blessing, the priest or bishop is quite often put at ease, knowing that the choir director will cooperatively work with him to ensure that the coordination of the liturgical details will be carried out appropriately. Anything that can be done to enhance mutual trust is to be embraced, and the giving of the liturgical blessing can go a long way to building that trust.

D. CONSTRUCTIVE COMMUNICATION

Establishing humility, obedience, and a bond of trust through the practice of giving the liturgical blessing, the main celebrant and the choir director now need to work out the details and liturgical specifics of the services through the use of an open and constructive communication. Again, with some priests and bishops feeling "out of their element" because of a lack of musical proficiency, they may seem initially uncomfortable discussing liturgical details with someone who is very much at home with both the liturgical services and the musical hymnology with which those services are celebrated. Here, the choir director needs to practice some pastoral compassion and patience, gently working and communicating openly with the celebrant to ensure that the director's expertise in musical matters does not appear overwhelming or liturgically threatening to the celebrant. By communicating in a manner that is open, gentle, honest, above-board, and informed (both the choir director and the main celebrant are well-trained and versed in the specifics of the services), the director can show the celebrant that having knowledge does not necessarily mean having control, domination, or power, but means that both persons can intelligently and efficiently work out the details and directives of the services so that the various ministries of the services are celebrated cooperatively and in unity.

This system of open communication, however, needs to be a two-way endeavor. If the main celebrant is the person who is to determine the liturgical specifics of a given service, then he needs to be open, honest, and clear about those specifics and communicate these directives to the choir director. To make a sudden change in a service while failing to communicate this change to the director and then expect him or her to assume what is going to happen or to somehow read the mind of the main celebrant is patently unfair. It takes very little effort to explain and instruct a director on any liturgical changes or differences that will occur that day. If, for instance, a set of icons is to be prayed over and blessed near the end of the Divine Liturgy, the celebrant needs to inform the director of this added event, specifically outlining that the people will sing "Blessed be the Name of the Lord" twice, then the prayers and blessing of the icons will take place with the appropriate responses, and then, finally, as the clergy reenter the sanctuary, the people will sing the third and final rendition of "Blessed be the Name of the Lord". There are times when such events come about last-minute, so to speak, as with the blessing of specific items such as icons. However, most special events are known well in advance, such as receiving new catechumens into the parish community (whereby a specific prayer is chanted and responded to at the beginning of the Litany of the Catechumens) or celebrating a baptismal or matrimonial Divine Liturgy. Since these circumstances are known weeks or even months before the events take place, it is fitting and appropriate for the celebrant to advise the choir director of the event **well in advance**, and to give sufficient allotted time to go over the specifics of the service with the director, as well as giving the director ample time to organize the musical elements of the event and successfully prepare his or her choir with plenty of rehearsal time available. If the celebrant fails to do this and things do not go well with the special liturgical event, then the celebrant has no one to blame for this but himself. Well-planned advisement, communication, and directives, however, will maximize the possibility that the celebration of the special liturgical event will go smoothly, peacefully, and joyfully.

    Such open communication can immensely help build a rapport and a relationship of trust and mutual respect that can be both beneficial to the parish community and enjoyable to both the choir director and the main celebrant for years to come.

E. THE EXPERTISE OF THE CHOIR DIRECTOR

One final word needs to be said, this time from the perspective of the choir director. While the director needs to be humble, obedient, and cooperative in regards to the authority of the main celebrant for the decisions of celebrating the liturgical services, the main celebrant needs to be mindful and respectful, as well, of the expertise of the choir director. Many people, even Church singers and choir members, have no concept of the long training, preparation, and practice of skills that is needed to be an effective and proficient choir director. Especially when a director has a very relaxed and smooth directing style, many people come to the erroneous conclusion that this ministry is exceedingly simple, needs hardly any training, and that just about anyone who can carry a tune can easily get up in front of the singers and direct the liturgical hymnology. Nothing could be further from the truth! As the information and examples presented in this book show, it takes a *lot* of time, effort, and slow, patient hard work to master the various skills necessary to become a worthy minister of Orthodox liturgical music. While being the person who specifically makes Christ present in the parish community and has the prerogative of making the final decisions regarding the services, the main celebrant also needs to acknowledge the training and expertise, musical, liturgical, and otherwise, of the choir director, and be open to constructive feedback and suggestions regarding the celebration of the liturgical services. Again, with both parties living a life of prayer, repentance, and humility, an open, loving, and constructively working relationship can be established and deepened between the main celebrant and the choir director, so that the specifics of the liturgical services may be worked out peacefully and efficiently, in order for these services to be celebrated "decently and in order".

ANSWERS TO EXERCISES

3. TRIADIC HARMONY

1.

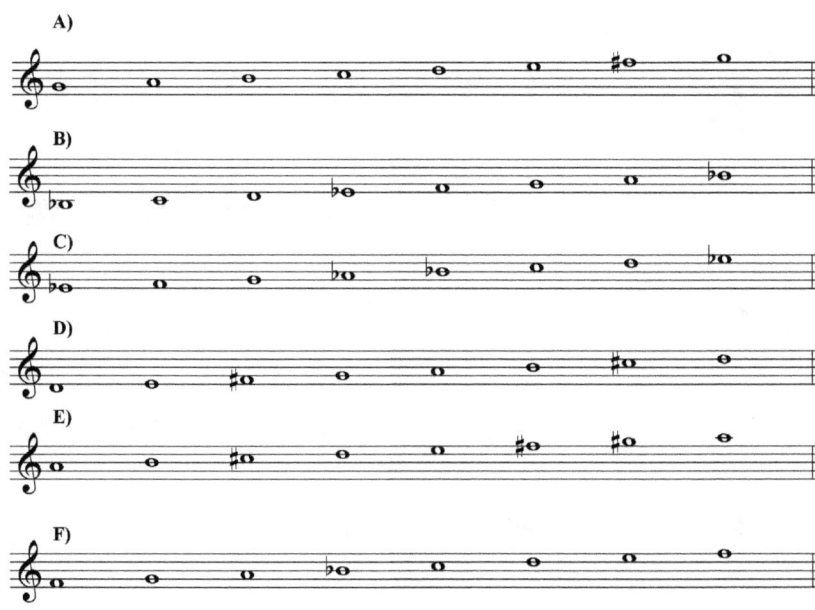

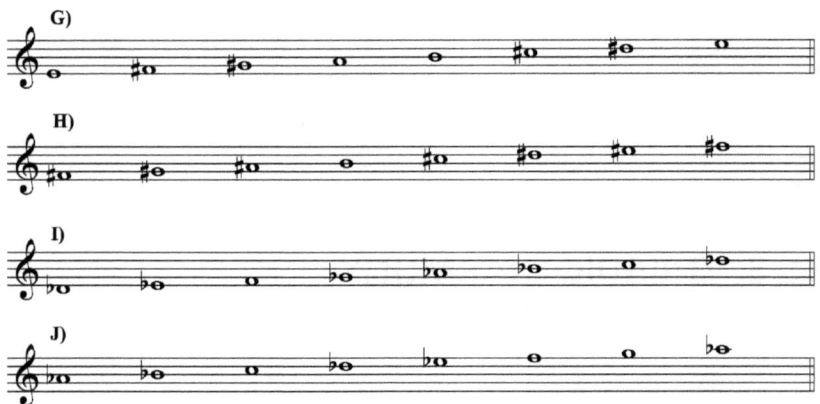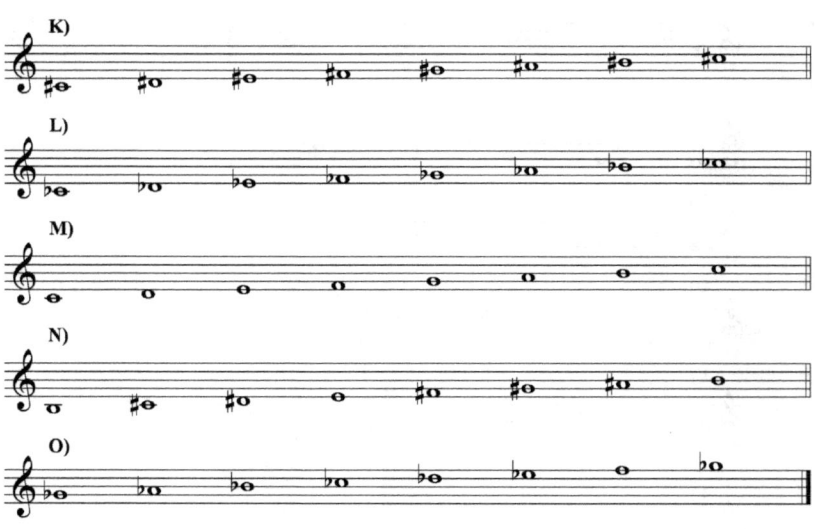

Answers to Exercises

2.

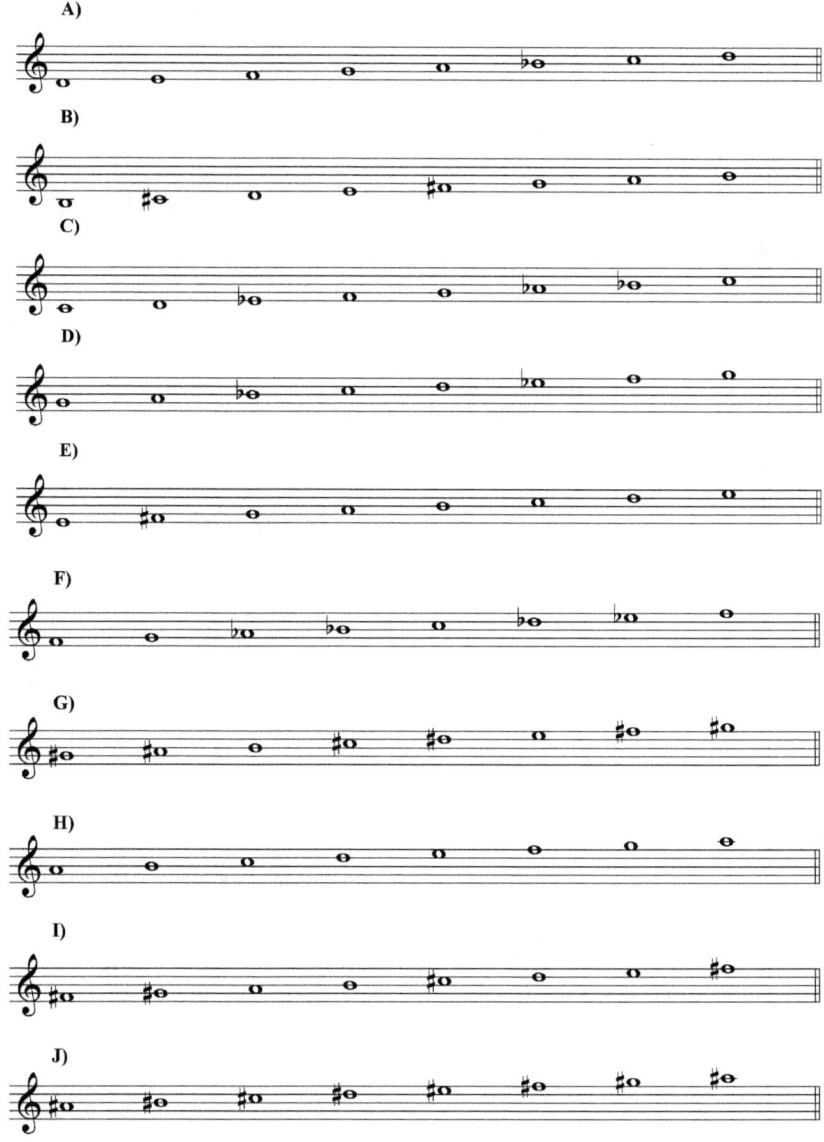

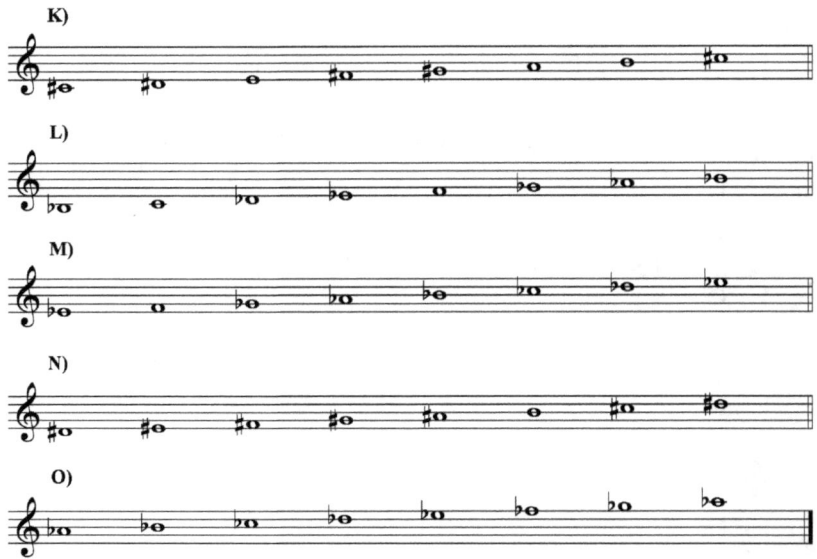

3. **W**hole, **W**hole, **H**alf, **W**hole, **W**hole, **W**hole, **H**alf.

4. **W**hole, **H**alf, **W**hole, **W**hole, **H**alf, **W**hole, **W**hole.

Answers to Exercises 237

5.

A)

B)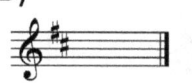

C)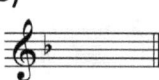

D)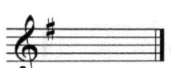

E)

F)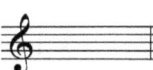

G)

H)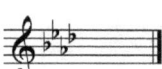

I)

J)

K)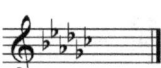

L)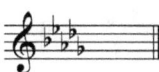

M)

N)

O)

6.

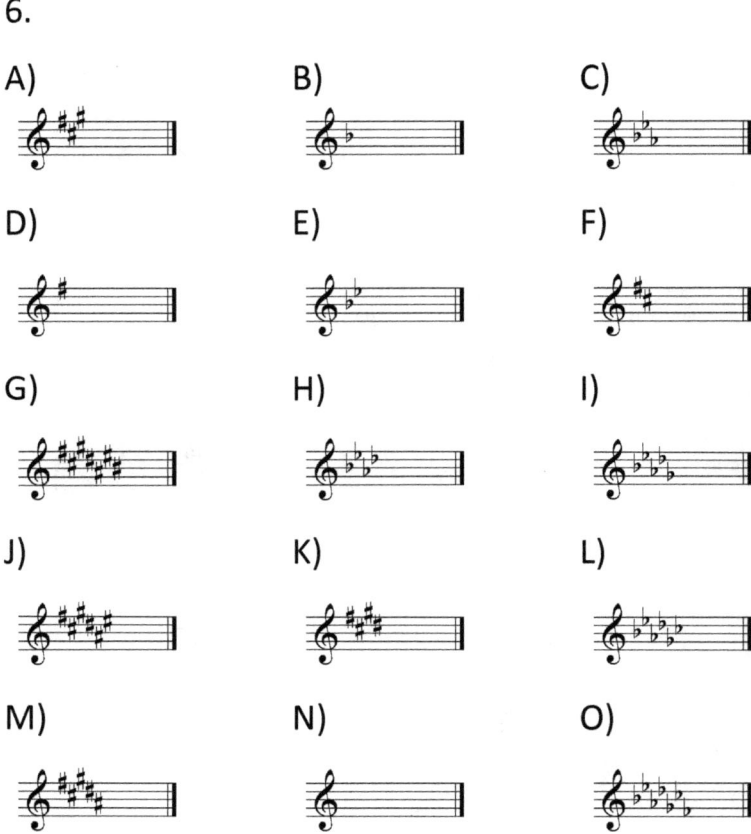

Answers to Exercises

7.

A)	E^b	B)	D	C)	A
D)	$G^\#$	E)	G	F)	D
G)	E	H)	E^b	I)	B
J)	$D^\#$	K)	E^b	L)	$C^\#$
M)	$F^\#$	N)	B^b	O)	G
P)	F	Q)	$C^\#$	R)	A
S)	G	T)	E		

8.

A)	d	B)	a	C)	e
D)	e^b	E)	g	F)	d
G)	a^b	H)	f^b	I)	b
J)	$g^\#$	K)	e	L)	a
M)	d^b	N)	a	O)	$c^\#$
P)	$f^\#$	Q)	e^b	R)	$f^\#$
S)	g	T)	g^b		

9.

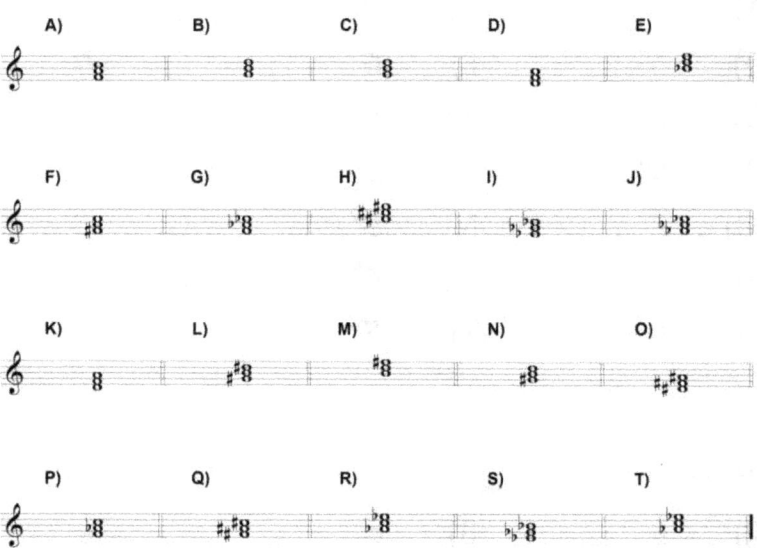

10.

A) major 3rd, minor 3rd, perfect 5th.
B) minor 3rd, major 3rd, perfect 5th.
C) minor 3rd, minor 3rd, diminished 5th.
D) major 3rd, major 3rd, augmented 5th.
E) major 3rd, minor 3rd, minor 3rd, perfect 5th, minor 7th.

Answers to Exercises

11. If, going from the bottom up, there is a major 3rd between the root of the chord and the 3rd, a minor 3rd between the 3rd and the 5th, and a perfect 5th between the root and the 5th, you have a major chord.

12. If, going from the bottom up, there is a minor 3rd between the root of the chord and the 3rd, a major 3rd between the 3rd and the 5th, and a perfect 5th between the root and the 5th, you have a minor chord.

13. In the following, the voicings for tenor, alto, and soprano may vary, as well as the octaves for any of the voices. What are important are the notes in the chord and which note is in the bass.

Answers to Exercises 243

14. In the following, the voicings for tenor, alto, and soprano may vary, as well as the octaves for any of the voices. What are important are the notes in the chord and which note is in the bass.

15. In the following, the voicings for tenor, alto, and soprano may vary, as well as the octaves for any of the voices. What are important are the notes in the chord and which note is in the bass.

16.

Take the tonic note of the major key, that falls on ***Do***, and go to the note that falls on ***La***, and you have the relative minor key. Or, take the note that falls on ***Do*** and go back two notes, and you have the relative minor key. For example, in ***F*** major, ***F*** falls on ***Do***. Go either to the note that falls on ***La*** or go back two notes from ***F***. In both cases, you come to ***D***. Therefore, the relative minor key from ***F*** major is ***d*** minor.

17.   I, ii, iii, IV, V, vi, vii°, I.

18.   i, ii°, III, iv, v, VI, VII, i.

BIBLIOGRAPHY

Music

Christ, William; DeLone, Richard; Kliewer, Vernon; Rowell, Lewis; and Thomson, William; ***Materials and Structure of Music, Volume 1***, 2nd Edition, Prentice Hall, Englewood Cliffs, New Jersey, 1972. Introductory material presented on a college freshman language level.

Jones, George Thaddeus, ***Music Theory***, Barnes and Noble (Harper and Row), New York, New York, 1974. Easier reading than ***Materials***, but not as complete.

Lamb, Gordon H., ***Choral Techniques***, William C. Brown Company, Dubuque, Iowa, 1976. Written for teaching singing in schools, it is nevertheless helpful, especially in the area of rehearsal technique.

Rudolf, Max, The *Grammar of Conducting*, 2nd Edition, Schirmer Books, Macmillan Publishing Company, Inc., New York, New York, 1980. The most complete conducting book written, both for choral and instrumental music.

Liturgical Music

von Gardner, Johann, *Russian Church Singing, Volume 1: Orthodox Worship and Hymnography*, St Vladimir's Seminary (SVS) Press, Crestwood, New York, 1980. A must for all liturgical musicians, it presents the structure and rubrics of the services of the Orthodox Church, as well as examining the essence of liturgical music.

Wellecz, Egon, *A History of Byzantine Music and Hymnography*, 2nd Edition, Oxford at the Clarendon Press, Oxford, England, 1980. The authoritative work on Byzantine chant.

Douglas, Winfred, ***Church Music in History and Practice***, Charles Scribner's Sons, New York, New York, 1937. Written by a Protestant, it is a valuable book on liturgical singing, particularly in the relationship of music and text.

Theology

Hopko, Father Thomas, ***The Orthodox Faith: An Elementary Handbook on the Orthodox Church***, Department of Religious Education, Orthodox Church in America, New York, New York, 1971. Written in four volumes (***I: Doctrine***; ***II: Worship***; ***III: Bible and Church History***; ***IV: Spirituality***), this series presents the teachings of the Orthodox Faith in a clear, easy-to-read format that is very understandable. Illustrated.

Schmemann, Alexander, ***Introduction to Liturgical Theology***, SVS Press, Crestwood, New York, 1986. A deep book that should be re-read many times, it is, however, invaluable for a correct perspective of the liturgical situation in the Orthodox Church.

Ware, Archimandrite Kallistos (Timothy), ***The Orthodox Church***, Penguin Books, New York, New York, 1963. A thorough handbook of the Orthodox Church, it discusses its history, faith, and worship.

Music Books

Drillock, David; Erickson, John H.; and Erickson, Helen Breslich, eds.; ***The Divine Liturgy***, SVS Press, Crestwood, New York, 1982. Contains settings of hymns for the Liturgy from various traditions. Also by SVS Press are: ***Holy Week: Volumes 1, 2, and 3***; ***Pascha: The Resurrection of Christ***; and ***The Liturgy of the Presanctified Gifts***.

Liturgical Books

Hapgood, Isabel Florence, ***Service Book of the Holy Orthodox-Catholic Apostolic Church***, 4th Edition, Syrian Antiochian Orthodox Archdiocese, Brooklyn, New York, 1965. Although the translations are quite archaic, the book does present all the services of the Church.

Nassar, the late Reverend Seraphim, ***Divine Prayers and Services of the Catholic Orthodox Church of Christ***, Antiochian Orthodox Christian Archdiocese, Englewood, New Jersey, 1979. Also archaic in textual usage, it nevertheless presents the rubrical propers of the liturgical services.

Ware, Archimandrite Kallistos and Mother Mary; ***The Festal Menaion***, Faber and Faber, London, England, 1969. Texts of the Twelve Major Feasts.

_____ ; ***The Lenten Triodion***, Faber and Faber, London, England, 1978. Texts of Great Lent, from the Sunday of the Publican and the Pharisee to Holy Saturday.

Liturgical Theology

Schmemann, Alexander, ***For the Life of the World: Sacraments and Orthodoxy*** (reprinted 2001), SVS Press, Crestwood, NY.

_____ , ***Of Water and the Spirit: A Liturgical Study of Baptism*** (1974), SVS Press, Crestwood, NY.

_____, ***Great Lent: Journey to Pascha*** (revised edition 1974), SVS Press, Crestwood, NY.

_____, ***The Eucharist: Sacrament of the Kingdom*** (1987), SVS Press, Crestwood, NY.

GLOSSARY OF TERMS

alla breve - also called ***cut time***, it refers to a time signature consisting of two beats per measure, with a half note getting one beat.

anacrusis - also called a ***pick-up note***, it is the beginning beat of a musical composition that does not begin on the first beat of the first full measure.

antecedent-consequent phrases - phrases which call for an answer; the antecedent phrase is the "question phrase", and the consequent phrase is the "answer phrase".

antiphonal singing - literally meaning "against the sound", it usually designates the use of two choirs in alternation.

augmented interval - a major or perfect interval that has been augmented (enlarged) one half step.

augmented triad - a triad consisting of two major 3rds and an augmented 5th.

bar line - the vertical line that separates one measure from another.

basic beat (duration) - the total time span from the beginning of one beat until the beginning of the next beat.

bass clef - also called the **F-clef**, it is the symbol at the beginning of the bass staff.

bass staff - the lower staff of the grand staff, which covers the bass range of voices, those of tenors and basses.

beat - a rhythmic pulse.

cadence - a musical ending or closing section.

cantor (canonarch) - a lead singer or reader.

chant - song; repetitive liturgical melody in which as many syllables are assigned to each tone as required.

chant style - a conducting style utilizing a combination of different meters, organized according to the text.

Glossary of Terms

chord - a group of three or more alternate pitches, sounding simultaneously.

chord tones - notes belonging as members of a chord.

clef - the symbol at the beginning of a staff that identifies that staff.

common time - a time signature consisting of four beats per measure, with a quarter note getting one beat.

conducting plane - the area in which the conductor moves his or her arms.

contour - the shape of a phrase.

cut time - also called **alla breve**, it refers to a time signature consisting of two beats per measure, with a half note getting one beat.

diminished interval - a minor or perfect interval that has been diminished (reduced) one half step.

diminished triad - a triad consisting of two minor 3rds and a diminished 5th.

dogma - an official teaching of the Church.

dominant - the tone a 5th above (or a 4th below) the tonic.

dotted note - a note with a dot following it, whereby the value of the note is increased by one-half.

downbeat - the first half of a beat, when the foot tapping the rhythm is going down to the floor.

drop preparation - a preparation beat used when beginning a hymn on the last half of a beat.

dynamics - the variation and contrast in the force and intensity (volume) of music.

eighth note - a type of note composed of a blackened (filled-in) note head, a stem, and a flag, which, in common time, takes up one-eighth of a measure in $\frac{4}{4}$ time.

eighth rest - a rest shaped like the number 7 and, in common time, takes up one-eighth of a measure in $\frac{4}{4}$ time.

Glossary of Terms

enharmonic - refers to two notes which are the same in pitch but have different letter names.

Eschaton - the Last Things; the Fulfillment of all in the Kingdom of God, which is ***eschatological***.

F-clef - also called the ***bass clef***, it is the symbol at the beginning of the bass staff.

The Father - He Who is God, Who is the Source of everything, both within the Holy Trinity (the Son and the Holy Spirit) and in creation; the First Person of the Holy Trinity.

first inversion - a chord with the 3rd in the bass.

Fixed Do system - the solfege system used primarily in Europe, where **C** is fixed as always being **Do**, no matter what key the music is in.

flat - a musical symbol that lowers the pitch of a note by one half step.

4-pattern - a conducting pattern in which 4 beats are conducted in the following directional pattern: down, left, right, up.

free meter - the meter of the chant style of conducting, in which the music is not confined to the regularity of one strict meter.

G-clef - also called the ***treble clef***, it is the symbol at the beginning of the treble staff.

God - the one God of the Christian Faith, the God of Abraham, Isaac, and Jacob, the Father Almighty, Who, by His very Nature, has a Son and a Holy Spirit.

grand (great) staff - the combination of the treble staff and the bass staff into one staff.

half note - a type of note composed of an open (not filled-in) note head and a stem, which, in common time, takes up one-half of a measure in $\frac{4}{4}$ time.

half rest - a rest which looks like a right-side-up hat, and which, in common time, takes up one-half of a measure in $\frac{4}{4}$ time.

half step - the smallest interval used in most Western music.

harmony - the chordal or vertical structure of a musical composition.

The Holy Spirit - the Spirit of God, Whose Personal characteristic it is to give Life to everything, even to God Himself; He is equally divine with the same Nature as the Father and the Son; the Third Person of the Holy Trinity.

homophony - music consisting of a single melodic line with harmonic accompaniment.

hymn - in general, any piece of liturgical song; specifically, a liturgical song whose poetic text offers praise or prayer to God.

interval - the distance between two tones.

intonation formulae - a pattern of notes or tones which function, most often, as a preparation or announcement of the mode of the melody of a Byzantine tone; if it comes between verses, it serves to link the recitation of the preceding verse with the verse that follows.

inversion - redistribution of chord tones out of root position.

ison - a repeated pitch that functions as a reference tone in Byzantine chant, to which the melody refers.

kanon tones - tones set to the texts of kanons, which occur primarily in Matins.

key - the tonal center of a Western musical composition.

key signature - the set of sharps or flats at the beginning of a musical composition.

leading tone - the tone a half step below the tonic, which leads up to it.

ledger line - a line above or below a staff on which to write notes.

liturgical - something which is, by its very nature, an element of the services of the Church.

liturgy - "common work" or "common action"; the central, eucharistic service of the Orthodox Church.

Glossary of Terms

lower interval - an interval that moves down from a given note.

major interval - interval of a 2nd, 3rd, 6th, or 7th that occurs naturally in the major key of the root of the chord.

major scale - a scale whose pattern of whole steps and half steps is: **W**hole, **W**hole, **H**alf, **W**hole, **W**hole, **W**hole, **H**alf.

major triad - a triad consisting of a major 3rd, a minor 3rd, and a perfect 5th.

measure - a grouping of the rhythmic pattern of a musical composition into a cycle of a specified number of beats.

mediant - the tone between (the "medium" or halfway" tone) the tonic and its dominant (halfway between 1 and 5).

melody - the horizontal set of pitches organized in time that determines the shape of a musical line.

meter - the grouping of beats.

metered music - music that is grouped in a specific number of beats.

middle C - the ***C*** on the ledger line between the treble staff and the bass staff.

minor interval - interval of a 2nd, 3rd, 6th, or 7th that occurs naturally in the minor key of the root of the chord.

minor scale - a scale whose pattern of whole and half steps is: ***W***hole, ***H***alf, ***W***hole, ***W***hole, ***H***alf, ***W***hole, ***W***hole.

minor triad - a triad consisting of a minor 3rd, a major 3rd, and a perfect 5th.

monophony - music consisting of a single melodic line without additional parts or accompaniment.

Movable Do system - the solfege system used primarily in the United States, where ***Do*** moves to the tonic of each major key.

motive - the smallest distinctive melodic germ, made up of a few tones and rhythm.

music - sound and silence organized in time.

natural sign - a musical symbol that cancels a sharp or flat.

octave - the space (distance) between two notes of the same letter name; interval of an 8th.

Oktoechos - the "book of the eight tones", it is used in all musical traditions of the Orthodox Church.

passing tone - non-chord tone that moves by step between two different chord tones.

perfect interval - interval of a 1st, 4th, 5th, or 8th (octave) as it occurs naturally in the major key of the root of the chord.

phrase - the smallest complete melodic unit that can stand alone.

pick-up note - also called an *anacrusis*, it is the beginning beat of a musical composition that does not begin on the first beat of the first full measure.

pitch - the highness or lowness of a sound resulting from vibrations per second.

plagal tones - tones (or modes) that correspond to another tone (or mode) whose number is referred to.

polyphony - music consisting of two or more independent melodies or lines.

preparation beat - a conducting signal to the singers which lets them when and how fast the music will begin, and that this is the moment to breathe.

prokeimenon - meaning "introductory hymn", it serves to introduce the theme of the Epistle and Gospel lessons.

prokeimenon tones - tones set to the texts of the prokeimenon.

quarter note - a type of note composed of a blackened (filled-in) note head and a stem, and which, in common time, takes up one-fourth of a measure in $\frac{4}{4}$ time.

quarter rest - a rest shaped like a zig-zag, and which, in common time, takes up one-fourth of a measure in $\frac{4}{4}$ time.

recitative - reciting pitch; the pitch in the middle of a phrase on which are sung many words or syllables.

relative minor - the minor key that shares the same key signature as a corresponding major key.

rests - musical signs that denote silence.

root - the basic tone that serves as the generating force for other tones in the chord.

root position - a chord built with the root in the bass line.

rubrics - meaning "written in red", it refers to the descriptions and specifics of the structure of services; originally written in the service books in red ink.

SATB - designation for four-part singing, it refers to sopranos, altos, tenors, and basses.

scale - a series of ascending and descending tones, arranged in a pattern.

scale degrees - numerical names for the tones of a scale that classify their particular function within the scale.

second inversion - a chord with the 5th in the bass.

7th chord - a chord of four alternate pitches, consisting of a root, a 3rd, a 5th, and a 7th.

sharp - a musical symbol that raises the pitch of a note by one half step.

solfege syllables - the set of syllables for sight-singing: *Do, Re, Mi, Fa, Sol, La, Ti, Do*.

solfege system - the system for using the solfege syllables for singing.

The Son - the eternal Son, Word, and Image of God, Who is the very Expression of the Being of the Father, and Who became incarnate as the man, Jesus Christ; the Second Person of the Holy Trinity.

staff - the set of lines and spaces on which music is written.

staves - the plural of "staff".

stikhera - verses.

stikhera style - a style of conducting stikhera that involves the use of the recitative and the cadence.

stikhera tones - tones used for the stikhera of such propers as "Lord, I Call" and the Apostikha at Vespers.

strict meter - meter having a strict number of beats for each measure.

sub-dominant - the tone a 4th above or a 5th below (the "under dominant") the tonic.

sub-mediant - the tone between (the "medium" or "halfway" tone) the sub-dominant and the tonic (halfway between 4 and 8).

subtonic - the 7th scale degree when it is a whole step below the tonic.

supertonic - the next tone above the tonic.

tenor - sustaining part.

theology - words adequate to God; the experience of our Faith, lived out in liturgy and in our daily lives.

third inversion - a 7th chord with the 7th in the bass.

3 pattern - a conducting pattern in which 3 beats are conducted in the following directional pattern: down, right, up.

time (meter) signature - the set of numbers at the beginning of a musical composition, showing how many beats there are per measure (the top number) and what type of note gets one beat (the bottom number).

tonic - tone of focus for the scale; the "home tone" of a key.

treble clef - also called the **G-clef**, it is the symbol at the beginning of the treble staff.

Glossary of Terms

treble staff - the upper staff of the grand staff, which covers the treble range of voices, those of sopranos and altos.

triad - a chord of three alternate pitches, consisting of a root, a 3rd, and a 5th.

troparion - a hymn whose theme is a specific saint or feast.

troparion tones - tones that are used to sing the troparion and kontakion, both resurrectional (for Sunday) and sanctoral (for the various saints and feasts).

2-pattern - a conducting pattern in which 2 beats are conducted in the following directional pattern: down, up.

upbeat - the second half of a beat.

whole note - a type of note composed of an open (not filled-in) note head without a stem, and which, in common time, takes up the whole measure in $\frac{4}{4}$ time.

whole rest - a rest which looks like an upside-down hat, and which, in common time, takes up the whole measure in $\frac{4}{4}$ time.

whole step - two half steps.

woodshedding - the gradual dissecting of the music down to its problem areas.

www.ingramcontent.com/pod-product-compliance
Lightning Source LLC
Chambersburg PA
CBHW050104170426
43198CB00014B/2451